Lillian J. Johnson Copyright © 2022

This e-book is licensed for your personal satisfaction only. This e-book may not be re-sold or given away to other people. If you would like to share this book with additional person, please purchase an additional copy for each person. If you're reading this book and did not purchase or buy it, or it was not purchased for your use only, then please return to Amazon.com and buy your own copy. Thank you for esteeming the hard work of this author.

All rights reserved. No portion of this book may be repeated, stored in a reclamation system, or conveyed by any means – electronic, mechanical, photographic (photocopying), recording, or otherwise – exclusive of prior permission in writing from the author.
ISBN: 979-8-36224-303-6

TABLE OF CONTENTS

ACKNOWLEDGEMENTS	9
FOREWORD	13
INTRODUCTION	20
CHAPTER 1	27
UNDERSTANDING SECOND JOBS	27
SIDE HUSTLES	31
HUSTLES ON MY SIDE	41
CHAPTER 2	56
THE PRE-HUSTLE PLAN	56
FULL-TIME WORK: WOULD YOU SAY YOU ARE INCREASING WEALTH?	59
ABSTAIN FROM WASTEFUL SPENDING	70
TRULY CHECK YOUR DEPT OUT	76
VOLUME–HOW MUCH DO YOU HAVE?	83
CHAPTER 3	92
TRACKING DOWN THE RIGHT SIDE HUSTLE FOR YOU	92
"SPEEDY MONEY" VERSUS "LONG TAIL MONEY"	95
LOCATION-INDEPENDENT VERSUS LOCATION-DEPENDENT	105
"PLANNED" WORK VERSUS "NON-PLANNED" WORK	112
HOW YOUR WAY OF LIFE & RELATIONSHIPS COME INTO PLAY_	119
CHAPTER 4	131
SPEEDY MONEY SIDE HUSTLE	131
WORKING RETAIL	134
FOOD DELIVERY	136
WAITING TO TABLES	138
OTHER PART-TIME JOBS	140
PRODUCT ILLUSTRATING	144
MYSTERY SHOPPING	147
CONTRIBUTING PLASMA	150
CHAPTER 5	156
ONLINE SIDE HUSTLES	156
PUBLISHING CONTENT TO A BLOG (BLOGGING)	158
SELLING ON ETSY	163
VIRTUAL HELPER	167
SOCIAL MEDIA MANAGEMENT	170
FLIPPING THINGS ON EBAY OR CRAIGSLIST	173
GRAPHIC DRAWING (DESIGN)	177
CREDIT CARD STIRRING	181
OPINION-GIVER (PROVIDER)	184

- PODCASTING 186
- MAKING YOUTUBE VIDEOS 189
- CHAPTER 6 192
- SMALL BUSINESS SIDE HUSTLES 192
- CREATING AN ONLINE PRODUCT TO SELL 194
- CREATING A PHYSICAL PRODUCT TO MANUFACTURE AND SELL 198
- LAUNCHING A WEB-BASED SEVICE 203
- WEDDING-RELATED PRODUCTS AND SERVICES 207
- ACCOUNTING & TAX SERVICES 212
- CHAPTER 7 215
- SELF-EMPLOYMENT SIDE HUSTLES 215
- SOVEREIGN/FREELANCE WRITING 217
- WEB ENHANCEMENT 220
- DATABASE COUNSELING 224
- PROGRAMMING 227
- PHOTOGRAPHY & FILMMAKING 230
- CHAPTER 8 235
- LOCAL SIDE HUSTLES 235
- DOGGISH WALKING 237
- PET OR/AND HOUSE SITTING 241
- CHILD CARE 245
- RENTING PLOT 249
- DELIVERY DRIVER 253
- TEACHING/INSTRUCTING 257
- REFFING SPORTS 260
- COACHING SPORTS 263
- MOVING SERVICES 269
- CHAPTER 9 272
- UPSIDE - THE UNEXPECTED GAINS 272
- THE BENEFIT OF CONNECTIONS 276
- NEW ABILITIES THAT SUPPORT WITH YOUR 9-5 283
- FINANCIAL CERTAINTY 286
- AFTER DEPT: HOW SIDE HUSTLES CAN LIFTOFF YOU AHEAD FINANCIALLY 290
- HIGH LEVEL SIDE HUSTLE POTENTIAL 294
- CHAPTER 10 298
- SIDE HUSTLE HACKS 298
- SKILLS TO FOCUS ON FOR N SUCCESSFUL SIDE HUSTLE 301
- ONLINE DEVICES THAT ASSIST WITH SIDE HUSTLES 311
- TIME HACKS FOR SIDE HUSTLES 318
- SECOND JOBS AND DUTIES: HOW TO GET READY FOR ASSESSMENT TIME 322
- CHAPTER 11 326
- ARRANGING EVERYTHING 326
- STAYING WITH A SIDE HUSTLE 328
- HAVING A STRATEGY PRIOR TO BEGINNING 330
- KNOW WHEN TO STOP 336

WHAT IS BEING SACRIFICED WHEN YOU QUIT A SIDE HUSTLE? 339
HOW MIGHT YOU CHANGE/ADJUST YOUR SIDE HUSTLES? 342
CONCLUSIVE NOTE 345

Dedication

Dedicated to the Hungry Mind!

ACKNOWLEDGEMENTS

To say the least, the period I was composing this book through was tempestuous. Nonetheless, too much reliable, proficient, and dependable people encompassed me, and I acclaim God for that. My Better half Johnson, who has been my incredible and dear companion for right around twenty years, merits exceptional acknowledgment. He has been an immovable mainstay of trustworthiness, consistent quality, support, help with this present reality, association, and persistence during the years that we spent composition, which continued all through everything under the sun else that happened in our life, regardless of how earnest or huge.

My folks, Jef and Elizabeth, my girl, Mikhaila, were okay there with me, giving close consideration, participating in a careful conversation with me, and supporting me as I sort out my words, contemplations, and deeds. The equivalent can be said for my sister Bonnie, who is generally dependable, and my remarkable microchip planner brother by marriage Jim Keller.

For a long time, both Michael and Joan

fellowship and Bilkis Cunningham's secretive and repressed help have been of incomprehensible worth to me. The foreword to this book expected definitely more work than I had expected, and Dr. Benjami blew away recorded as a hard copy and reconsidering it.

    My whole family is appreciative for the benevolence and warmth that he and his better half, Esther, reliably stretch out to us. Working with my supervisor at Mexico house, was a pleasure. A considerably more estimated and adjusted work came about because of Craig's careful meticulousness and capacity to delicately get a grip on enthusiastic explosions of feeling (and sometimes disturbance) in my various modifications. Before my book was even composed, my companion and individual Guide Pinky Recky used a few of my life standard, which was an enormous commendation and an indication of their expected worth and fame. While I was composing and altering, Ricky chipped in as a gave, fastidious, furiously sharp, and cleverly critical proofreader and reporter. He helped me with wiping out pointless language and keeping up with the story stream. Ricky furthermore proposed David Smith, who made the beautiful illustrations that open every part. I might want to say thanks to him for that as well as offer my appreciation to Ethan himself, whose delineations bring genuinely necessary warmth, fun loving nature, and daintiness to what might somehow have been a too desolate and sensational book. At last, I'd need to offer my thanks to Mrs. Sarah Johnson, who fills in as both my representative and a brilliant partner. This book could not have possibly been composed without Nazify.

FOREWORD

My most memorable lemonade stand, I have been dealing with the side. Secretary, remote helper, individual colleague, career expo leader, coat checker, distributer of flyers, theater instructor, I've filled in as a sitter and an examination subject. In reality, I've I have never acted in a "traditional" way. utilized".

However, nowadays, my side business is not any more portrayed by odd occupations paying $10 to $20 an hour going about as a monetary security net My hustle has since developed from an endurance one. strategy for a firm with an about six-figure yearly income.

Nonetheless, let me to console you that this example of overcoming adversity isn't It's anything but a commitment; it's simply my experience.

I can't guarantee that your side business will be productive.

I can't ensure that you will find a calling you appreciate

I can't ensure that your hustle will bring about a benefit.

However, it is conceivable. It has for myself and numerous different hawkers who have roused my side hustle experience - here is the reason...

Side hustling is an open door - an opportunity to be deliberate, enhance, and oversee your procuring potential; an opportunity to begin taking care of obligation, increment your retirement investment funds, and meet your monetary targets; an opportunity to build a daily existence in your own particular manner!

For my purposes, the side work addressed a valuable chance to break liberated from the pattern of win and fail that I'd become used to as an expert entertainer in New York City. At first propelled by endurance, I side hustled to earn barely enough to get by my costs till the following acting task It was, in any case, obliged.

I started to think more extensive about my endeavors in the wake of becoming exhausted of late evenings shutting at the café followed by early morning tryouts. It was a fine technique to get by till tomorrow, yet it was anything but a way to develop the existence of my fantasies.

I preceded with my café, looking after children, individual help tasks to earn a living wage, however I likewise began composing with laying out something more reasonable and versatile.

My underlying excursion into paid composing got me $20 per piece, which wasn't quite a bit of an expansion in pay, so I moved myself to request more. At the point when clients wouldn't arrange, I searched for new ones who might. Gradually however consistently, the requests became bigger - $30, $50, $100, $500, $2,000 - and the payouts followed behind. So enormous, truth be told, that it turned out to be in excess of a second job for me. I likewise had a subsequent work.

There was no single wonderful second, no lightning strike that helped the value of my new side hustle by 100, just the steadiness of hoping for something else from myself, my work, and my clients.

Side hustling is about strengthening: outfitting improved procuring potential to give you more other options and carry your optimal life nearer to the real world. To understand your most prominent potential, you should move past the demeanor of momentary endurance and seek after the hustle antic, insane goals that regularly live just in your mind.

Making fantastic signals rejuvenates these deceptions, if by some stroke of good luck in words. When clearly impossible dreams could turn into a reality on the off chance that you keep on asking noisily and give esteem in light of those solicitations.
This was my old mantra:

"six-figures by thirty," I'd share with my accomplice as I left to get dry washing for somebody I was helping or take the train out to Jersey for a youngster I was looking after children. Today, I'm 29, and notwithstanding all chances, my maxim is turning into my world.

This book contains the demeanor changes and down to earth strategies you'll have to accomplish similar outcomes. You'll figure out the significance of a second job, get clear ideas on the most proficient method to lay out your own, and start utilizing the best practices to drive you in the clear financially and into monetary freedom.

I comprehend that going out and strolling another person's dog, cleaning another person's home, or changing diapers on another person's kid may not appear to be fabulous or pivotal at the time, but rather on the off chance that you start the cycle and focus on your second job with the power and aim of making something as large as your most extravagant fantasies, you might end up finding a way that opposes each breaking point you thought existed and opens ways to potential open doors you never viewed as conceivable.

Good luck hustling.

INTRODUCTION

My husband and I wedded soon after we moved on from school.

We were eager to start our coexistences as love birds and youthful school graduates. We needed to buy a house, obtain our graduate degrees, and travel. One thing stressed both our relationship and our funds: the around $100,000 in school obligation we owed.

The $1,000+ installment we paid on our understudy loans every month was a critical channel on our assets. More awful, these were insignificant installments; going on like this, we'd be paying $1,000 out the entryway consistently for the following decade.

It's implied that having such a lot of cash go towards school obligation every month was crippling. All it's challenging to follow your goals when you never appear to have "enough" cash.

In spite of my situation in corporate bookkeeping, understudy loan obligation, joined with life's different commitments, left a huge opening in our post-graduate funds. While headways at my normal everyday employment might be useful, they don't come around frequently. Consistently, I had practically zero a potential open door to bring in additional cash at my 9-5 works.

My experience isn't exceptional. More than 70% of late school graduates have understudy loans, and the typical 2015 college alumni has developed somewhat more than $35,000 in the red.
The aggregate sum of educational loan obligation outperforming $1.2 trillion of late. That is reason enough not to strain individual financial plans, but rather likewise a whole economy.

Regardless of whether an understudy has no buyer or charge card obligation when they graduate, the weight of educational loans can smash. Numerous twenty to thirty year olds are finding themselves incapable to seek after their post-graduate desires.

As an individual budget blogger, I've seen a few pieces about how individuals could forestall or pay off educational loan obligation.

These postings might be valuable for secondary school understudies simply beginning school, yet what might be said about people who have recently graduated and have a lot of understudy obligation?

Reducing expenses is one choice. This methodology has various allies. In all actuality, however, uses must be decreased up until this point. A cost-cutting estimate Normally doesn't let loose sufficient cash to make a critical impact on funds and furthermore requires a decrease in way of life.

As opposed to zeroing in on reducing expenses and making troublesome way of life transforms, I feel that zeroing in on delivering more cash is the best way for people who are in the red.
"How unequivocally do I get more cash-flow?" is the conspicuous request that people ask accordingly.

I offer a preferable choice over the run of the mill strategy for zeroing in on creating more cash at your 9-5: side hustles.

When I say "second job," many individuals

typically say, "Huh? "What precisely does that mean?" Having a side business just suggests having a type of revenue other than your 9-5 work in your extra time While you might not have whole command over how much cash you make at work, you really do have unlimited oversight over how much cash you make beyond work.

I've had many side hustles over the past ten years. They range from working an end of the week occupation to writing for a blog on evenings and ends of the week. No matter what the range of part time jobs I've embraced, they all shared one thing practically speaking: they generally gave a critical lift to my cash.

To get a poker relationship, since moving on from school, I've bet everything on part time jobs. From independent composition to what I term "accounting sheet counseling," I've done everything. While each second job included enormous penance, the advantages they conveyed couldn't possibly be more significant. The cash I've made in my extra time has assisted with school obligations, vehicle installments, and different costs.

While I have no designs to stop my 9-5 work and seek after one of my second jobs as a calling, I know many individuals who have done as such. It's only one of numerous unforeseen advantages of having a part time job.

Hustle Away Obligation will direct you through the method involved with beginning a fruitful second job that will build your pay, assist you with taking care of obligation quicker, and carry on with a superior life, from picking the right part time job for you to giving you thoughts for side hustles you can begin to investigating the unforeseen (and wonderful) advantages of having a side hustle.

Now is the right time to hustle away dept.

CHAPTER 1

UNDERSTANDING SECOND JOBS

For the beyond five years or something like that, I've worked in corporate money. During this period, I worked a great deal with Microsoft Succeed and gleaned tons of useful knowledge about bookkeeping sheets. All things considered, in the event that you work on calculation sheets for 4-8 hours every day, 5 days per week, you're probably going to significantly improve at them, particularly assuming you're in a section level job looking for ways of sticking out.

Yet, what do calculation sheets in an office desk area have to do with second jobs?

As a matter of fact a lot.

A couple of years prior, a companion of mine who works a private venture called me and said he wanted some help with his organization's monetary calculation sheets, and my name was quick to ring a bell. Following the conversation We waited to a portion of the issues and hardships that his bookkeeping sheets were causing him, as well as how may be bettered his documents.

He additionally showed that he had saved assets for this undertaking. As a new college alumni with a few understudy loans, I got at the opportunity to enhance my pay beyond my regular work. Bringing in extra cash was not the sole advantage of this work; I was likewise leveling up skills that would be valuable at my everyday work. One more benefit of the hustle was that it very well may be done from a distance and at whatever point it fit my timetable.

That is the manner by which my "Spreadsheet Consulting" second job got everything rolling.

Accounting sheet consultancy is one illustration of how side hustles might assist you with enjoying surprising benefits There will be erring on this later in the book.
I haven't done any bookkeeping sheet counseling in a couple of years, yet I have been dealing with a couple of opposite side undertakings. Later in this section, I'll go

through my side hustles in general and how they've turned out for me. However, before I get into my opposite second jobs, we should talk about side hustles overall. All things considered, this might be your most memorable prologue to the subject.

SIDE HUSTLES

Second jobs are techniques to enhance your standard pay. For instance, when I was dealing with a companion's calculation sheets, I was likewise counseling for him in the nights and on ends of the week. It was It was anything but a substitution for my full-time compensation, however it was a method for enlarging it.

The way that second jobs are profoundly unique is a significant thought to get a handle on. They can be basically as straightforward as a seasonal work done in the nights and on ends of the week, or as modern as planning an item in China and selling it on the web.

Side hustles could occur during customary business hours or whenever. They might be area free (i.e., you can be perched on your couch in your nightdresses) or request your genuine presence. They could consume 3 hours or 30 hours of your recreation time. Insofar as the work falls inside the boundaries of A second job is characterized as "bringing in cash notwithstanding a 9-5 compensation."

Perceive your "Why"
Individuals participate in side hustles for various reasons. They are as per the following:

STUDENT LOANS
A huge number of school graduates are burdened with educational loan obligation. I fell into this gathering on the grounds that both my better half and I graduated with huge understudy loan obligation. Our $1,000+ per month understudy loan installment drove my quest for part time jobs, including the making of YoungAdultMoney.com. I didn't maintain that my way of life or targets should endure because of our school obligation, so I set off to compensate for any shortfall with additional income.

OTHER DEPTS

Purchaser obligation, contracts, and different obligations could likewise push individuals to chase after work beyond their 9-5. A great model is somebody who has a vehicle credit and is exhausted of causing extra obligation each time they purchase a vehicle. They may either sit and groan or they can do activity. One proactive step they might take is to utilize second jobs to take care of their vehicle advance quicker and begin setting aside cash for their next car in real money.

CATEGORICAL FINANCIAL AMBITIONS

A reasonable financial goal to hold back nothing individuals to lay out a side business. We should investigate something that many individuals can connect with: travel. Accept you need to travel yet your present monetary condition doesn't permit you to bear the cost of the get-aways you need to take. Bringing in Cash procured notwithstanding your 9-5 occupation could produce a subsequent income stream committed to travel.

Home enhancements are another great

model. Accept you can save $500 every month for house enhancements. That suggests you'll have $6,000 following a year. Any individual who claims a home comprehends that $6,000 doesn't go far with regards to home enhancements. A holding wall might cost somewhere in the range of $5,000 to $20,000, and that is only for the wall! On the off chance that you can acquire an extra $1,000 each month from second jobs, you might expand your regularly scheduled installments to your home enhancements record to $1,500, which compares to $18,000 each year.

WIDENING OF REIMBURSEMENT
Nearly everybody has been laid off from a task or is familiar with undoubtedly another individual who has been laid off With our economy's new win fail cycle, as well as how quickly innovation and new businesses upset entire organization areas, having a supplemental pay source is more critical than any other time. There is no such thing as a protected calling or area.

I'm not suggesting that a side hustle will unavoidably supplant your full-time pay (however it's an engaging possibility for some), yet having even a little measure of cash rolling in from an optional pay source could give a security net on the off chance that your significant pay source is lost. There are additionally a few part time jobs, for example, writing for a blog, that don't pay anything for the initial 6 a year. At the point when you have a second job, it is impressively more straightforward to get start when you live it up compensation instead of when you really want cash immediately.

ENTREPRENEURSHIP
There are many individuals out there who are business visionaries yet work a 9-5 occupation because of multiple factors. I'm one of those people. Second jobs have empowered me to explore in the little organization region without endangering my reliable and unsurprising 9-5 check.

Part time jobs empower individuals to lay out an organization without facing the entire challenge of depending totally on it for money. Incredible on the off chance that it succeeds! In the event that it comes up short, by and large only a tad measure of cash is lost, if any. While a side hustle business visionary might lose time spent to a bombed second job, When a "full-time" business person's firm falls flat, the monetary misfortune is typically not as serious.

Understanding your "why" is basic with regards to part time jobs. In the event that you persevere with side hustling for quite a while, there will be times when you get back home from work in the wake of a monotonous day and don't have any desire to do anything, not to mention work more. This is one of the less engaging components of side hustling and will compel you to ponder your "why" to keep propelled.

As recently expressed, my "why" is for the most part understudy loan obligation. I don't need the $1,000 each month we spend towards school obligation to restrict my monetary choices. I need to have the option to travel, buy a house, and do all the other things I fantasized of achieving in my twenties and thirties.

I'm likewise spurred by a craving to broaden my pay and an innovative tingle. In an ideal world, I would claim my own business or, at any rate, have unlimited authority over both the work I do and my day to day daily practice. Try not to misunderstand me: there are numerous phenomenal positions out there, and nothing bad can really be said about having a vocation, however most occupations don't fulfill a pioneering inclination. Luckily, we live in when there are more choices than any other time to lay out and work a business in your extra time.

HUSTLES ON MY SIDE

Regardless of my enthusiasm for business, I have never filled in as a full-time business person or entrepreneur. I have Since secondary school, I've had some work and worked.

My chief kind of revenue has forever been as a worker. With school credits, it's for all intents and purposes unfathomable for me to stop my work and become a full-time organization proprietor. Might you at any point picture the weakness of not having a consistent pay? A great many people who have school credits or other obligation have thought about this. Maybe some of you perusing this are as of now organization proprietors, however for numerous others, and myself the chance of passing on a regular task to seek after an enterprising undertaking is a (monetarily) overwhelming idea.

There are, fortunately, side hustles. Many side hustles might develop into everyday positions or organizations. For That is a profoundly engaging an open door for business visionaries.
Benefit of a specific second job.

1) WORKING FOR A PART-TIME JOB
I filled in as an understudy laborer in my college's IT division all through school. It was a magnificent work, yet I need more. During my first year of school, I had my most memorable side hustle: a seasonal work.

On Friday nights and Saturdays, I worked for office furniture moving firm. We moved individuals' crates of possessions when they changed work areas. We'd likewise move whole desk area segments and dump semi-trucks stacked with gear.

This was an amazing second job since it was adaptable regarding timing. You might pick the decision about whether to work each end of the week as long as you informed the scheduler by Wednesday. On the off chance that you would have rather not or couldn't work, not an issue I was likewise ready to team up with quite possibly of my dearest companion. It's a piece more straightforward to surrender part of your end of the week to produce cash when you can enjoy it with quite possibly of your dearest companion.

2) WORK FOR A BLOG
Dealing with a blog was another way I enhanced my pay. During my undergrad years, I met an individual accounting blog proprietor by chance through a political blog I established. We eventually began conveying, and I wound up doing blog stuff for him consistently.

This was a marvelous work for me since I got openness to the functional component of writing for a blog and created huge abilities in business, promoting, and different things like inquiry enhancement of the motor It furnished me with proficient experience for my CV and massively helped me when I eventually sent off my very own money webpage, Youthful Grown-up Cash.

3) WRITING FOR A BLOG

I started composing almost a long time back with a political blog. I at last started writing for a blog for a political gathering blog too. It was a decent opportunity for growth, yet I brought in no cash from it, so it was anything but a genuine side business. My political writing for a blog days were best depicted as a "enthusiasm try."

I sent off Youthful Grown-up Cash in July of 2011. In spite of distributing 5-6 times each week, observing virtual entertainment accounts, and doing every one of the significant things, I didn't earn a cent for the initial seven months how you should make a fruitful blog

I ultimately began creating cash from publishing content to a blog in 2012 and have been doing so from that point forward. From that point forward, I've had the option to utilize essayists and re-appropriate piece of the work to save time for things like composing this book. Writing for a blog isn't "difficult" cash, however there are numerous parts of publishing content to a blog that make it an engaging side work. More on it in a second.

4) POKER
"Pause, poker is essentially betting!" that is the very thing some of you might think. You couldn't realistically be endeavoring to convince me that poker is a side hustle!" If it's not too much trouble.

Hold on for me.

All through school, I played poker consistently, both on the web and face to face at card rooms. I never had an enormous result like a modest bunch of my secondary school colleagues (one prevailed upon $300,000 in a solitary occasion and one more won more than $200k in another), yet I made a smidgen of side cash from playing.

While some (or most) poker players will lose cash over the long haul, while I began playing, there were more players with normal to less than ideal abilities. Individuals who viewed the game in a serious way and had better than expected capacities had the option to produce cash after some time.

5) ACCOUNTING SHEET NOTICE (SPREEDSHEET CONSULTING)

I recently referenced my accounting sheet counseling experience, which I actually view as quite possibly of the best part time job I've at any point had. While it required that I penance time for cash, It permitted me to rehearse an expertise that I use at work while likewise permitting me to work from anyplace I picked (at home, cafés, and so on.).

One thing I gained from my second job is the means by which tedious it is to part time job. In my extra time, I couldn't want anything more than to perform more bookkeeping sheet counseling, however I simply don't have the capacity. I likewise attempt to zero in on side hustles that can possibly be even more a detached kind of revenue as opposed to ones that request you to exchange your time for a foreordained measure of cash.

6) PART-TIME COMPOSITION (FREELANCE WRITING)

Independent writing is one of those part time jobs that a lot of people need. Who, all things considered, would have zero desire to sit at home the entire day drinking espresso and composing?

Tragically, therefore independent writing is a particularly cutthroat industry. The benefit of independent writing as a side business is that you are not subject to the income. You don't really "need" to take each work that comes your direction, and losing a client isn't so horrendous as it would be assuming it was your only wellspring of income.

My blog assisted me with getting a couple of independent writing position. I had an extremely high least I charged per piece and might have taken on extra tasks at a decreased rate, but since it was my side pay, I could be particular and just take more lucrative tasks.

7) PARTICIPATING IN GIVEAWAYS
Many individuals are surprised when I let them know that I used to enter sweepstakes as a second job. They don't think "winning things" is a genuine technique to produce

cash. Regardless, my significant other and I entered large number of prizes throughout the span of two years. During that time, we even had a Friday "Giveaway Gathering" piece on my site where we featured 100-300 awards that wrapped up during the next week.

We had the option to bring in some pleasant cash by winning odd things, for example, a vehicle seat, a kitchen sink, a kid's shelf, a $400 yard trimmer, passes to the MLB Elite player game, and different awards gift vouchers, in addition to various different things We sold nearly all that we won and transformed it into cash. a certifiable second job.

I keep on entering a portion of the bigger sweepstakes. I accept it is beneficial for you to put shortly to a great extent setting your name in the cap. You simply never know!

8) RENTING A ROOM IN OUR HOME
My significant other and I obtained a house with a storm cellar loft a couple of years prior and have leased it essentially the entire time we've had it. It's been a dynamite side

hustle, as the additional cash has assisted make with lodging proprietorship more sensible. We've invested some parcel of energy previously, during, and after tenants have lived there.

So rental cash is a long way from a 100 percent automated source of income. Having that month-to-month lease check, then again, has made it worth our time, particularly on the grounds that we are continually looking for new strategies to create side cash to help us take care of obligation.

As you might be aware, I've endeavored different part time jobs.
Ideally, you'll concur that nothing on my rundown is strange - I didn't make an organization that sold for a huge number of dollars, nor did I plan a totally new item that is sold everywhere. To side hustle, you don't need to do anything insane or new; it very well might be just about as fundamental or complex as you like.
 Probably, you have a couple of thoughts for second jobs that you accept you'd cherish chasing after, yet you'll simply have the

option to investigate a couple of them Because of time requirements, I couldn't seek after those thoughts. The advantage of part time jobs is that they assist you with taking care of obligation speedier, save more, and get more cash flow.

Putting away cash rapidly permits you to focus on and investigate second jobs that are conceivably more hazardous (for example starting a business that will not be productive for over a year) yet maybe really fulfilling (selling the business for $10 million!).

CHAPTER 2

THE PRE-HUSTLE PLAN

Concerning the subject of how best to get to the powerful your financial situation, there are two camps in the singular spending plan world. The chief camp acknowledges reducing expenses and it is marvelous to continue with a more efficient life approach, while the resulting camp truly thinks extending pay is the best system. By far most fall a few in the center between these two cutoff points.

While this book is essentially revolved around extending pay, it would be senseless not to look at a piece of various ways to deal with work on your assets preceding taking the side hustle course.
In light of everything, there may be a basic and judicious ways to deal with further foster your assets that you haven't endeavored.

Considering these decisions preceding

starting a side hustle is ideal since once you start a second work it will in general be difficult to find the opportunity or energy to seek after them.

In this segment, we'll focus in on three things: your continuous everyday employment, your continuous money related situation (like spending penchants and commitment), and your capacity to concur with on a specific position hustle.

FULL-TIME WORK: WOULD YOU SAY YOU ARE INCREASING WEALTH?

This book is connected to acquiring cash despite your regular employment, so what's the point of messing with examining your 9-5? There's one huge inspiration to focus in on your 9-5: it very well may be broadly less complex to get more income at your 9-5 than it will be to at first get cash at a subsequent work.

We ought to use a manual for frame this point. Jennifer works 20 hours seven days, reliably, endeavoring to get cash composing for a blog. Jennifer could get through 6 a year making in a don't real sense anything, and subsequently $500 each month, ultimately $1k+ consistently. Regardless, when Jennifer comes to the $1k+ a month level, the compensation can vary in any case requires Jennifer to relinquish hustle antic proportions of her spare an open door to keep the compensation coming in.

Assume Jennifer capabilities as an Exhibiting Inspector at a huge venture for her ordinary work. Jennifer wouldn't worry the work and has had extraordinary reviews the past two years. She's very pleasant in her current work environment and inclinations people she works with. Besides she stays busy with her blog and has been getting some money on it, so she's not in a huge rush to take on another situation with another gathering.
So she stops.

In addition, stop.

How might Jennifer answer? How should you answer?

 We ought to expect Jennifer is prepared for a more significant level at work. She's "normal" as some would concur, and could by and large with no issue find a Senior Advancing Inspector work. We ought to in like manner hope to be the compensation raise would be an extra $10k each year.

I think you see where I'm going with this.

On the off chance that Jennifer some way or another ended up start applying and chatting with for occupations at a higher level, she would likely land one in something like a short time. We ought to moreover expect she wouldn't work longer hours. Positively, she might have more noteworthy commitment, yet in various corporate positions - especially at non-boss levels - by far most work equivalent hours whether they are at section level or focus the leaders. By climbing, she would make more money yet would have compelling reason need to relinquish any additional time.

Finding another profession at a more significant level would simply intensify the impact of her temporary work. She would obtain more from her regular occupation while at this point getting a comparative total from her second job.

She can continue to direct her side hustle towards commitment and use the extension in her regular compensation for venture assets, travel, or anything that she needs.

There are many work conditions where you will realize that you should get remunerated more. Nevertheless, how might you know definitely? I propose every delegate should regularly finish two things:
look at work open doors and really investigate GlassDoor for pay data.

LOOK AT BUSINESS VALUABLE OPEN DOORS

One thing that I do something like once reliably or two is look at business valuable open doors for a more elevated level at work. I see what kinds of capacities fall into the fundamental region and which fall into the leaned toward region. I see what sort of confirmations and establishment data enrolling chiefs are looking for. I see what particular and sensitive capacities they need.

I don't simply consume this information. I

change it into critical things. In case a larger piece of the positions are looking for people who have worked with data, I would consider contributing to projects that anticipate that I should address and separate enormous educational assortments. I could attempt to contribute energy past work constructing these capacities (preferably through a second job).

I figure everyone should reliably look at business open doors for positions quite a while before they truly expect to seek after another position. This gives time to the design up of capacities and gaining the significant experience that organizations are looking for.

The best likely increase of looking at business open doors is that there is an opportunity you could comprehend that you are prepared for a more lucrative position.

TRULY CHECK GLASSDOOR FOR SALARY DATA OUT

One site that I propose people visit something like once everybody very few months is GlassDoor. GlassDoor has massive proportions of remuneration data as well as studies of associations by both current likewise, past delegates.

How a GlassDoor function is it grants clients to scrutinize at first the site, yet finally keeps them from overview additional information until they register and purposely offer up their remuneration information. There is no bet in presenting pay information in light of the fact that the data they show to general society is absolutely obscure and gathered.

GlassDoor can be inconceivably essential to laborers who are unsure whether they are getting remunerated a market rate. For model, I work in the cash division at a hustle antic organization. As you can imagine, there are numerous people at a similar level with a comparable title as me. On GlassDoor I can see the extent of point by point pay rates as well as the typical. Accepting for the time being that I'm getting remunerated $5,000 not the very typical, I can positively address my executive about attracting my pay closer to the ordinary.

You can examine loads of associations on GlassDoor and even channel for your specific geographic region. You could attempt to figure out that a comparable circumstance at another association pays basically more than your association. Given that this is valid, it might be an ideal opportunity to examine a move.

As frequently as conceivable looking at business potential open doors and doing pay research isn't conventional direction, and by far most perhaps do it when they expect they are ready to apply and chat with for another position. Make an effort not to be simply person! Also, guarantee you regularly update your resume and LinkedIn. Nobody can tell whenever an open door will come your course.

Assuming the best of all worlds, you will really need to extend the amount of money you make at your 9-5 and a short time later beginning a second occupation to increase your compensation extensively further. Growing your 9-5 compensation isn't by and large possible, be that as it may, or may be limited in light of residency, association system, and the kind of work you do.

In case you're stretched to the edge from a compensation perspective at your 9-5 yet need a more significant salary, a seasonal occupation is a phenomenal decision for growing your compensation.

ABSTAIN FROM WASTEFUL SPENDING

While this book is based on getting more money to deal with commitment and continue with a prevalent life, it's key to basically go through some time studying and considering approaches to overseeing cash beforehand going with the decision to start a side hustle.

To frame this, we ought to include Ted for example. Ted is an energetic capable who lives and works downtown. He goes through about $1,500 a month renting a space in a stylish area. He moreover routinely eats out for most meals - not to determine progressive happy hours.

Notwithstanding having a solid job for a 20-something, Ted is fighting to pay his $800 month-to-month student credit bill on top of all his various expenses.

By and by assume Ted decided to review his spending. For a considerable length of time, he recorded all his spending and put it into an estimation sheet. He was paralyzed to find that he spends more than $1,000 on diners and refreshments consistently. Likewise his rent what's more, utility costs were making up a colossal piece of his spending. He wasn't saving or contributing a great deal and was really living check to check.

Taking into account this news, Ted decides to move to a suburb where there are more rental decisions and tracks down a one-space for $800/month, generally not the very $1,500/month he was paying midtown. He starts to convey a lunch to work and scales back how habitually he goes out to dinner.

Ted may be a ridiculous model, but the truth

of the matter is this: if you're fighting with commitment, one of the essential exercises is review your spending. A large number individual don't normally follow their spending thoroughly for two reasons: they are uneasy at what they will find and it will in general time-consume.

Following your spending a while and reviewing how much your compensation will each spend order can be instructive for some. For others, there may be no shocks.

In case there are districts you can downsize, it most likely looks at to carry out the improvement. In case you are centered around starting a second job, you could have the choice to grow your spending in those locales not excessively far off. In light of everything, temporary positions should give an open door with the objective that you can choose to consume cash.

TRULY CHECK YOUR DEPT OUT

Not all commitment is same. There is a significant differentiation between high-interest Visa commitment and low-interest agreement commitment. The supporting expense on my home credit is 3.5% and I expect to take care of that development as relaxed as could be anticipated, simply in light of the fact that I'm gotten at a low rate.

Some singular financial plan bosses will instruct you to take care with respect to your commitment regardless of what the credit cost. I can respect this view assuming it comes as per the perspective that the psychological benefit of being sans commitment counterbalanced the upside of gripping low-interest commitment.

In this way, I think there is an extraordinary arrangement to be obtained from holding low-interest commitment and, as opposed to settling commitment speedier, creating save assets and theories. Anyway, that may be for another book. I vigorously recommend everyone with charge card commitment or student advances examine the top notch rate and their decisions for chopping their rate down and, thusly, chopping down the total they pay towards revenue.

CREDIT CARD DEPT
Over the top interest Credit card commitment can injure. Whether or not you still hanging out there to pay it down, there's a good open door that it will expect over a short time to discard it, meaning you will continue to pay a ton of interest instead of settling the standard.

There are two philosophies you can take to ease up a piece of the desolation of excessive interest Credit card commitment.

The first is to see as a 0% APR Visa that you can move the harmony to. These Visas give you a delight period - regularly a year - where you really want to pay no interest on the balance you move over.

Having this breathing room can be a hustle antic benefit to people who are doing combating with charge card commitment. Not only will it promptly set free some pay, it will in like manner license you an opportunity to take various steps towards settling up the commitment, like working a temporary work.

0% APR card offers change every now and again, so I won't propose any unequivocal cards at this moment (you can continually take a gander at Energetic Adult Money for state of the art offers). Expecting you truth be told do embrace this technique, recall that some charge a one-time balance move cost to make the fundamental trade.

The resulting decision is to get a commitment mix credit. The supporting costs on these credits won't be outright base, yet they might conceivably bring the rate down from 20%+ to something like 10% (and at

55

times even lower). A Visa with a 0% APR move is the best decision yet if you don't meet all necessities for one, a commitment cementing credit may be a good discretionary decision.

UNDERGRADUATE CREDIT DEPT
I think each person who has student advance commitment is particularly mindful of the severe reality that there is no captivated recipe for getting liberated of it. While I think having a subsequent occupation can remarkably get to the powerful your ability to settle up student credits, it's valuable to discuss instructive advance reworking going before diving into part time job methods.

Student credit rethinking works like a home advance reevaluate. An association deals with your credits and sets you up with another credit at a lower advance expense. The benefit to the credit holder is the potential for colossal save supports if they revise at an out and out lower funding cost.

Student credit reconsidering isn't the most ideal thing on the planet everyone, as you genuinely lose a piece of the honors that go with student credits. One of those honors is having the choice to surrender your advances when you are in graduate regular day to day existence you face financial trouble. Make sure to research at these things before you decide to rework.

VOLUME-HOW MUCH DO YOU HAVE?

Having the cutoff concerning a seasonal occupation is huge. Second positions are characteristically irksome and exhausting because they are done on top of a regular work. Burnout is an evident opportunity.

Right when I consider limit, I for the most part review a conversation that was given at a one-day drive meeting that I went two or three quite a while ago. This organization meeting was based on staff and volunteers of various non-benefits. The speaker reached a significant decision about limit that has remained with me straight up to the current day.

Essentially what they said was that you ought to have the choice to say "no" to things and make limit regarding the things you center around. If you will start a subsequent work, do you have sufficient recreation time to truly get it moving? Do you truly need to eliminate something of your life to save the time and cutoff for your second job?

If your work days are currently jam-squeezed from 6AM to 11PM, might you at any point go to make a subsequent work? Do have opportunity and willpower on the closures of the week that you can use for your subsequent work?
Are there various obligations you can scale back or crash all around as far as possible regarding your subsequent work?

I know someone who truly quit their regular work giving lawful guidance allowed them close to no capacity to seek after a part time job or even have an entirely wonderful life past the workplace. It was normal everyone would come in and work on Saturdays and there was a lot of strain to put in more hours.

She hated the work and culture so she sought after a 9-5 work that was actually a 9-5. This gave her capacity to seek after her temporary work and overall made her significantly more upbeat with her work/life balance.

Realizing your needs is basic. To be sure, there are responsibilities to your ordinary work, your family, and others, but in the long run, if you're centered around dealing with commitment through side hustles, you need to zero in on them.

All through running Energetic Adult Money the past at least three
Years, I have expected to relinquish a ton of opportunity to create content, change content, advance the webpage, and the great many different things that go into running a powerful blog. There were various nights and closures of the week that were spent at home or coffee shops money management energy. It's been problematic once in a while yet being prepared to adjust my month-to-month student credit portions - and subsequently some - has put forth it totally worth the attempt.

Regardless, making this book anticipated that I should relinquish other entryways. I was set to begin the part-time MBA program at the School of Minnesota whenever the expected opportunity to form this book happened as expected. After wary idea, obviously this book was a more serious need than starting my MBA. Luckily I had the choice to yield enrollment until the going with semester.

Repentances for temporary positions are generally speaking significantly more unobtrusive than nonetheless, delaying a MBA. It could mean getting fairly less lay on weeknights, or communicating no to that second (or third) dream football affiliation. At last, expecting that you will make your side hustle a need and see that it won't constantly be quite easy to fit into your schedule, you obviously will undoubtedly win than someone who went in blind without initial considering the results. Coming up next is a certified plan you can use to guarantee you consider each possibility prior to pursuing a subsequent work:

THE PRE-HUSTLE PLAN

Explored potential for a more rewarding work
- Is it valid or not that you are prepared for a more rewarding work?
- Have you evaluated pay data on GlassDoor?

Followed and investigated pay and expenses
- Tip: Use a free compensation/cost following accounting sheet or program like Mint
- Where are you spending more money than you could like?

Cut down funding cost on commitment where possible
- Will your banks consider cutting down your credit cost?
- Does a 0% APR card appear to be all right? Is it an opportunities for you?
- Does a singular credit appear all right to consolidate exorbitant interest credit?

Investigated student advance reward decisions
- Might you anytime cut down your consistently planned portion through pay based repayment?

Now that we've finished the pre-hustle plan, lets get on to the horseplay stuff - finding the right second job.

CHAPTER 3

TRACKING DOWN THE RIGHT SIDE HUSTLE FOR YOU

The beneficial thing about part time jobs is that there are tons of choices. The terrible thing about part time jobs is that there are a lot of choices.

It's not difficult to stall out in "thought land" with regards to second jobs. When somebody begins contemplating beginning a side hustle, it's normal to come up with different thoughts they might want to seek after. Having more choices is definitely not something terrible, yet it turns into an issue in the event that it keeps you from making a move and really beginning a side hustle.

I think the cycle for beginning a second job is equivalent to the most common way of beginning a blog. There's a limitless number of themes, a limitless number of plans and a limitless number of decisions to make about a blog. A many individuals like beginning a blog, yet they don't quite execute their thought.

The main piece of a second job is really beginning. This part is tied in with tracking down the right second job for you. It won't assist you with choosing precisely which side hustle to begin, however it will assist you with recognizing which kind of second job best accommodates your way of life, character, and interests.

How about we get everything rolling with my thought process is the least demanding method for arranging side hustles: "speedy cash" versus "long tail."

"SPEEDY MONEY" VERSUS "LONG TAIL MONEY"

The reason of this book is beginning part time jobs to settle obligation quicker. Certain individuals might be in a frantic circumstance where they need cash quickly. On the off chance that you fall into this gathering, you will be in an ideal situation seeking after a "fast cash" second job rather than a "long tail" part time job.

Speedy cash is genuinely obvious: a second job furnishes you with cash quick. It is ensured side hustle pay, and it begins when you start your second job. One of the most incredible instances of a fast cash side hustle is conveying pizzas.

At the point when I worked at a pizza place in secondary school, there were a couple of drivers who just worked two or three hours every evening. They were individuals who had other regular positions however conveyed pizzas as an afterthought to enhance their pay. They loved the reliable compensation, the short weeknight moves that fit in the hours beyond their 9-5, and the way that the work was more physical than other 9-5s, like programming.

There are incalculable speedy cash second jobs. They include:
- Working at a retail location evenings/ends of the week
- Taking an occasional work around special times of year
- Coaching
- Secret Shopping
- Item Show
- Bartending

Speedy cash second jobs are great for individuals who need pay that is ensured, don't have any desire to go into business, and are happy with doing an alternate kind of work than they do in their 9-5.

This differentiations with what I call "long-tail" part time jobs. Long-tail side hustles don't ensure pay, commonly require a more innovative outlook, and might possibly transform into more work than was initially expected. On the in addition to side, long-tail side hustles offer a couple of extraordinary expected benefits: the chance of selling a business for a single amount, the chance of another profession, and the possibility to get much more cash long haul than a speedy cash part time job. Contributing to a blog is an exemplary illustration of a long-tail side hustle.

Bloggers can go 6 a year without making a dime, and may try and wind up losing cash. There is no assurance that a blog will at any point bring in cash. It additionally quite often requires more investment and exertion than individuals expect.

On the in addition to side, a productive blog can normally be sold for a singular amount. There is likewise the possibility to have it transform into a regular work, particularly in the event that the blog gets on and draws in peruses. Blog proprietors can likewise use their website to get independent composition and other "gigs." At last, contributing to a blog can be perfect for business visionaries who need to deal with a private venture in their extra time. It requires overseeing content (the item), expediting commercials, promoting, funds, and all the other things that an entrepreneur would experience.

Publishing content to a blog isn't ideal for everybody and is most certainly not by any means the only lengthy tail part time job choice. Some other long-tail side hustles choices are:

- Showing music examples
- Selling an item on Etsy
- Creating, assembling, and selling an item on the web
- Public Talking
- Occasion Videographer
- Representing an independent company
- Charge Arrangement
- Beginning a Webcast
- Turn into a YouTube character

- Modifications/Fitting
- Web-based Entertainment The board

There is most certainly a hazy situation while discussing fast cash versus long-tail second jobs. For instance, you could contend that mentoring is actually a long-tail part time job, as need might arise to lay down a good foundation for yourself and construct a standing and, thus, customers. However, you could likewise contend that coaching is a fast cash second job since there are organizations that recruit individuals to guide for hourly rates, and there is practically zero exertion expected to get clients.

No matter what all the ill-defined situation that accompanies arranging side hustles as either speedy cash or long-tail, the concentration ought to be as an afterthought hawker rather than the side hustle. Returning to the coaching model, it would check out for somebody who needs to fabricate their own mentoring business as an afterthought or potentially have more command throughout their time and pay to seek after the long-tail second job. If they need cash faster or essentially need to place in the hours and get ensured cash, they ought to rather seek after a coaching position at a laid out organization.

What we just depicted can be considered as far as the "roof" and "floor" of a part time job. In the event that you decide to convey pizzas as a side hustle, you will probably get extremely predictable part time job pay. The roof, or the most extreme you can make, won't be colossal, however the floor, or the base you can make, additionally won't be simply low. Basically, you are exchanging a low roof for an anticipated floor.

Presently on the off chance that you contemplate a side hustle that is more gamble based, for example, having items fabricated in China and sold through a site you made, you will have an unfathomably different roof and floor than the individual who decides to convey
pizzas as their side hustle. The floor would really be
negative for this situation, since you would need to put great many dollars into your organization without knowing
whether you will equal break even. The roof,

however, is
incredibly high since it could transform into an organization that creates heaps of income and can be sold for a lot of cash. I'll discuss high-roof side hustles in the Startling Advantages of Second jobs part, where I discuss financing more hazardous side hustles with stable side hustle pay.

LOCATION-INDEPENDENT VERSUS LOCATION-DEPENDENT

Side hustles are the same than "standard" positions or work as in there are area autonomous side hustles and area subordinate second jobs. The vast majority need to begin an area free second job for the very reasons that many craving area autonomous positions: they would rather not manage a drive, they need to work from the solace of their home, and they need command over their current circumstance.

I figure everybody can envision the advantages of having a area free part time job, so all things considered I need to zero in on the disadvantages that accompany an area autonomous second job. The greatest disadvantage is the more elevated level of rivalry. I will show this with a model from my 9-5.

Prior to changing to my ongoing 9-5 in corporate finance, I worked in corporate bookkeeping. Regardless of the way that we produce a virtual item and in a real sense everything the work is finished on a PC, everybody actually crashes into an actual structure to work every day.
While large numbers of my partners were astounded when we began reevaluating work to our "Worldwide Arrangements" unit in India, I was not. Since the work should be possible from a distance, I realize that I was contending with individuals all around the world for my work.

Relating this back to side hustles, it's vital to understand that with some area autonomous second jobs you will wind up rivaling individuals everywhere, and once in a while

74

it will make the part time job not worth the effort. For instance, I've considered accomplishing more calculation sheet fill in as a second job, yet it's extreme rivaling individuals abroad

who are charging very little each hour. Important once in a while not such a lot of the opposition powers individuals to stop area free second jobs, however the way that they are not dedicated to investing the energy after quite a while after-week without seeing reliable pay from their endeavors. A few things just call for additional investment and exertion before they are effective. A webcast or Youtube channel could require numerous months to develop an economical crowd.

Remember that it tends to be valuable to seek after an area subordinate second job in the event that there is area subordinate work you appreciate. For instance, there will continuously be interest for pet-sitting, house-sitting, dog strolling, finishing, giving music illustrations, food conveyance, bartending, and other work that requires the individual offering the assistance to be actually present.

One development region ready for area subordinate part time jobs is anything connected with the older/resigned segment. My grandparents have a parental figure who does numerous things for them that they can never again do, for example, going to the store for food and family things as well as well as errands around the house like food prep and cleaning. The resigned segment additionally needs essential innovation preparing. This is something that essentially any millennial can give and is wonderful to somebody who has a ton of persistence.

Another development region ready for side hustles is wellbeing and wellness. I know somebody who gives bunch wellness classes in the nights at a nearby exercise center. She appreciates driving the classes however doesn't do it as an everyday work. Individual preparation is another side hustle that wellbeing cognizant people should seek after. This could be transformed into an area free side hustle assuming you make a site that has gym routine schedules or recordings telling individuals the best way to do specific activities appropriately.

"PLANNED" WORK VERSUS "NON-PLANNED" WORK

One of the greatest advantages of a 9-5 is the anticipated hours. Ordinarily, for a long time and after quite a while after-week the hours are the very same. Pay is unsurprising. Simultaneously, this can likewise be one of the greatest drawbacks of a 9-5, as certain individuals work better late around evening time or are more useful in the event that they work a couple of hours, take a couple off, and continue work.

Since side hustles are finished notwithstanding 9-5 work, you enjoy one major benefit: picking whether to seek after booked or non-planned work. In the event that you like having a conclusive planned time span, there are numerous evening and end of the week occupations where you can work explicit movements. On the other side, on the off chance that you like to work at whatever point you need to - and not work when you would rather not - a part time job like independent composing may be great. At last, there are a few second jobs that have a combination of both, for example, a picture taker who has booked photograph shoots yet can alter photographs at whatever point (and any place) they need.

So which is better? Booked or non-planned work? Likewise with most things connected with side hustles, the response is "it depends."

Booked work is commonly simpler to find and more unsurprising (there's an explanation 9-5 positions are planned). In the event that you really want side hustle cash quickly and need it to be basically as predictable and dependable as could be expected, you more likely than not will need to search for planned work.

Work that doesn't need to be finished during explicit hours will definitely be less unsurprising from a pay stance, however it likewise might be more agreeable work. One explanation I love running a blog as a part time job is on the grounds that I can in a real sense do it at whatever point I need. Indeed, there is more rivalry than a few opposite part time jobs and income can be flighty, however I like having the option to work on it when I want to deal with it.

One more inquiry that surfaces is whether an item or administration is better. In the event that you have the opportunity and obligation to foster an item to sell, it could be a preferable choice over offering a support. A genuine illustration of this is Janet Kim of Keen Calculation sheets. She sells bookkeeping sheets she has created on her site SavvySpreadsheets.com. The decent thing about her second job is that she had the option to foster the bookkeeping sheets individually and needn't bother with to be genuinely present when a client buys her accounting sheets - the entire deals and conveyance process is mechanized through her site.

On the off chance that you are seeking after a more enterprising part time job, I would urge you to be available to the two kinds of work. Janet likewise offers calculation sheet counseling administrations. While this might require her investing explicit effort on her schedule to meet with clients, it's only another method for expanding and broaden the income of her side hustle.

One more genuine illustration of a side hustle that can be either booked or non-planned is resume and introductory letter counseling. Certain individuals are normally great at organizing and phrasing resumes and introductory letters. This could be either a planned or non-booked second job. It would be planned if half-hour or drawn out gatherings were set up with clients to survey and work on their resume and introductory letter. It would be non-planned on the off chance that you basically have clients present their resume and introductory letter and they are surveyed and returned as far as possible.

As a general rule, on the off chance that you want to bring in cash as quickly as possible to begin cushioning your ledger and settling obligation, consider a part time job that has planned work. Assuming you make them inhales room and can manage fluctuating and flighty pay, consider investigating a side hustle that doesn't work on a set timetable.

HOW YOUR WAY OF LIFE & RELATIONSHIPS COME INTO PLAY

All through this section, one thing ought to have become clear: the side hustle you pick should fit with your way of life and current financial circumstance. On the off chance that you're a spouse and father, it's essentially not sensible to have a second job that gets you far from your family each weeknight or consistently. Assuming that you're single, however, it turns into a choice.

For one of my dad's new birthday events, we went to an eatery to celebrate. As we were visiting with the server, we figured out that he waited to tables on evenings and ends of the week on top of possessing a finishing business. Between the two positions, he worked from 7am to around 10pm practically consistently. I expected he was single since, can we just be real, that kind of plan for getting work done is just practical on the off chance that you don't have family responsibilities.

In the event that you have a critical other or potentially kids, a tad
Inventiveness can go quite far with regards to side hustles. One system is to coordinate your family into your second job. For instance, while my better half is somewhat uninvolved with Youthful Grown-up Cash, she has contributed blog entries before and, surprisingly, set up a week-by-week giveaway post consistently for quite a long time.

I have another companion who has a photography second job. His better half currently second-shoots with him at weddings. Having your life partner work with you makes it somewhat more straightforward to legitimize forfeiting summer ends of the week to chip away at a second job. As a matter of fact, I know a couple of picture takers who have attempted this game plan and it can function admirably.

It's not simply family and relationship requests that can make it challenging to work a part time job. Many individuals have social, volunteer, schooling, leisure activities, travel, and different responsibilities that make it challenging to support a part time job.

There is no keeping away from the work that accompanies a second job. Regardless of whether you can fabricate a business that is area autonomous and that should be possible individually, there will constantly be work that must be finished if you have any desire to keep on bringing in cash next to you hustle.

Try not to attempt to consider the side hustle that will be the least conceivable work since you will likely wind up disheartened at the amount surprisingly work it is. All things considered, consider what fits best with your way of life and consider getting inventive to make your second job work with your ongoing obligations and responsibilities.

As you conclude which side hustle to seek after, remember that you can constantly pause and begin a part time job. All things considered, a side hustle ought to be to some degree pleasant since you are forfeiting your spare energy to make it happen.

Cheer up assuming you are right now in the camp that requirements to seek after a second job that turns out revenue right away yet wish you had the option to seek after a long tail part time job. You can constantly switch part time jobs when your monetary circumstance improves, which is unavoidable on the off chance that you are sufficiently roused to seek after a side hustle in any case.

Utilize the accompanying worksheet to assist you with getting everything rolling with tracking down the right side hustle for you.

PICKING THE RIGHT SIDE HUSTLE
List 3 of your side hubbies
1.

2. _____

3. _____

List 3 of your abilities
1. _____

2. _____

3. _____

QUESTIONS:
Could I at any point do a part time job connected with my side hubby? What might that resemble?

_____
_____
_____
_____

What issue could I at any point settle for individuals utilizing my abilities?

_____
_____

_____
_____
_____

How might I offer some benefit to other people?

_____
_____
_____
_____

Do I want cash as quickly as possible or could it seem OK to seek after a second job that might take more time to be productive?

_____
_____
_____
_____

Do I have to seek after an area free part time job or am I open to an area subordinate second job? How significant is this to me?

_____
_____
_____
_____

_____

Do I have to seek after non-booked work or am I open to planned work? How significant is this to me?

_____
_____
_____
_____
_____

List 3 part time job thoughts that sound interesting to you

1.
_____

2.
_____

3.
_____

CHAPTER 4

SPEEDY MONEY SIDE HUSTLE

Up to this point we've been centered principally around planning to begin a side hustle. Planning is vital, however what might be said about thoughts for explicit second jobs?

Throughout the following couple of sections, we will investigate a few thoughts for side hustles. These part time jobs range significantly by type. Some are area autonomous while others require being genuinely present. Some will essentially ensure reliable side pay, while others are possibly more worthwhile however may not work out.

There is some cross-over in the bucketing of side hustles, however I gave my all to place the part time jobs into legitimate classes in view of what individuals are searching for in a side hustle. Some might require cash rapidly, so the speedy money part time jobs area will give them thoughts of side hustles that will achieve this. Others may just craving a work-from-anyplace online part time job. The web-based part time jobs segment will be where they need to look.

There is a side hustle for everybody. There are in a real sense
great many open doors for part time jobs. These are a couple of thoughts to assist with your own conceptualizing. We'll begin by discussing fast money part time jobs. The ones that offer the fastest money normally include finding a part-time line of work. Taking on a seasonal work notwithstanding an everyday occupation can begin getting income as fast a long time.

WORKING RETAIL

Working a retail work is one of the speediest and most straightforward ways of making side hustle cash. There are endless retail locations in some random city with a hustle antic assortment of environments, hours, and necessities. There is likewise high turnover in retail so there commonly won't be a long meeting/on-boarding process.

Retail could be a simple method for working only a couple of hours a week, such as a Saturday shift or a couple weeknight shifts. It tends to be extremely obliging to the individuals who want to work rigorously night or end of the week shifts. Besides individuals are normally hoping to dispose of hours so there is generally an amazing chance to add more hours assuming that you need.

FOOD DELIVERY

Food delivery, similar to retail, is an industry that is ideally suited for individuals hoping to enhance their pay. It may not be the most charming thing to do in your extra time, however there is consistently interest for qualified drivers to work at night and end of the week hours.

My most memorable occupation was cooking at Pizza Cottage and I likewise worked at a pizza joint that is nearby to Minnesota called Pardon. At Pizza Cottage specifically, drivers got more cash-flow than the administrators. Conveyance drivers likewise are required most during supper rush, so there is potential to work only 2-3 hours at a time and gather some fair side pay.

WAITING TO TABLES

My sister waited to tables two or three summers notwithstanding her everyday work. There is an eatery in Minnesota that is situated on Lake Minnetonka that ordinarily draws in rich clients. In some cases she got more cash flow in her brief night shift than she did at her 9-5.

It's not difficult to Tend to tables. It very well may be upsetting, tiring, and baffling. It can - and will - be worth the effort, however, assuming that you are zeroing in on obligation reimbursement and other monetary objectives.

Like tending to tables, bartending is another help industry work that will continuously be popular. There are endless cafés that need servers and barkeeps, regularly at night and end of the week hours that are prime for individuals hoping to side hustle.

OTHER PART-TIME JOBS

Eateries and retail aren't the main businesses that proposition obliging second job temporary open positions. To give a couple of models:

OFFICE/WORK SPACE MOVER
As I referenced before, I made some part-memories work as an office/desk area mover. The movements were Friday evenings and Saturday mornings, yet just when I needed to work.

CHILD CARE
My better half worked at the YMCA for more than 10 years. She arrived at this extraordinary achievement by just never stopping her temporary work in Kid's Stuff. She kept on dealing with Saturdays all

through school and in any event, for a couple of years after school. It was a pleasant side pay source and the way that she partook in the work was a major reward. We were likewise ready to help a free exercise center enrollment through her business. Simply one more method for reducing month to month expenses.

CONCESSIONS AT A GAMES/SPORT STADIUM
Pro athletics offer an abundance of side hustles, from sports writing to occupations at the arena. I have various companions who have worked in concessions in their extra time at MLB games, as well as one companion who covers Minnesota sports as an independent essayist.

In the event that you need speedy, unsurprising, stable side pay, part-time occupations can be an extraordinary choice. They may not be essentially as captivating as a few opposite part time jobs, however they truly do frequently permit surprisingly adaptability and choices.

PRODUCT ILLUSTRATING

Being an item demonstrator can be perfect for anybody searching for a side hustle that has unsurprising compensation and doesn't need as much mental energy or exertion as opposite side hustles, like beginning an outsourcing business. It is likewise great for somebody not hoping to take on a seasonal work and really like to not be continually checked by a chief. You've presumably seen item demonstrators at different retail locations toward the end of the week.

Chonce from the blog My Obligation Revelation was an item demonstrator for a long time and she thinks this is quite possibly of the best second job out there. Beginning compensation is around $11-$13/hour and can be essentially as high as $20/hour. Moves ordinarily last somewhere in the range of 4 and 8 hours. It's sensible to make

$300-$500 in part time job cash consistently.

While certain retailers recruit item demonstrators to work in their stores, different retailers work with an organization that works in item exhibitions. Alcohol stores are a well-known place for item exhibitions, for self-evident reasons. My sister wined exhibitions previously and partook in the work. It's likewise important that liquor item demonstrators normally make more each hour than other item demonstrators.

MYSTERY SHOPPING

Mystery shopping is one more effective method for bringing in cash as an afterthought without taking on a temporary work. Certain individuals really track down shopping fun and would without hesitation take advantage of the chance to be paid to make it happen - I know, it's challenging for a few of us to comprehend!

Mystery shopping is generally direct. Organizations need input on their clients' shopping experience. To get that information, they are able to impetuses customers to give their criticism. Prompt mystery customers.

Once settled, you can do as numerous or as not many mystery shops as you need. Kristin from the blog Trust in a Financial plan says that the people who view it in a serious way can make two or three hundred bucks a month up several thousand every month. Kristi suggests MysteryShopForum.com for figuring out more about mystery shopping and iMysteryShop.com for getting shops.

The shops can shift in type. They can incorporate eating at an eatery, looking at another high rise, going to a wellbeing spa, seeing a film, or quite a few different things.

CONTRIBUTING PLASMA

Likely the most notable side pay source is giving plasma. Plasma is the protein-rich piece of the blood that conveys red and white platelets. Plasma is important for treatment of various intriguing sicknesses.

How much cash you can make giving plasma changes. It can go from the low finish of $10 per gift as far as possible up to $60 per gift. The primary visit regularly requires close to two hours as a wellbeing test is fundamental, yet after the main visit it ought to just require an hour to 90 minutes.

The Food and Medication Organization permits individuals to give blood/plasma two times each seven-day duration. On the off chance that you have tattoos you will most likely be unable to give. Numerous gift places are open later at night (for example until 8pm) so it functions admirably for individuals hoping to give notwithstanding a 9-5 timetable. A special reward is you are (in a real sense) saving lives by giving plasma. It can take many plasma gifts to make medication to treat one patient for an entire year.

PROVIDING CARE AND SENIOR ADMINISTRATIONS

As referenced before, there is a ton of interest for administrations for senior residents. As increasingly more people born after WW2 resign, there will keep on being an expanded interest for administrations for senior residents. Offering types of assistance toward the end of the week or nights is a choice, as it could offer full-time guardians a reprieve, or offer insignificant types of assistance to senior residents who are more free.

Getting things done like getting food and family products can assist old people with remaining in their own home. Also, administrations like cleaning, food prep, clothing, and giving transportation are everything that old people might require.

As a parental figure you could offer particular types of assistance, like just basic food item conveyance. Having only one help would permit you to cluster the work, for example, just making one supermarket run however looking for at least three clients. Remember different things that seniors might require, for example, PC preparing or assist incorporating new innovations into their home like web with overhauling.

CHAPTER 5

ONLINE SIDE HUSTLES

Online side hustles are part time jobs that should be possible anyplace there is a web association. Online pay has most certainly been worshiped for as far back as decade since, indeed, who would have no desire to bring in cash from the solace of their own home?

So, being practical when it is significant comes to online pay. It tends to be challenging to rival others for online pay essentially on the grounds that it's a particularly helpful method for bringing in cash.

Nonetheless, it is totally conceivable to bring in cash on the web on the off chance that you are adequately propelled. All things considered, almost 100 percent of my side hustle pay the beyond couple of years has come from online second jobs.

PUBLISHING CONTENT TO A BLOG (BLOGGING)

Publishing content to a blog 5 has been my essential wellspring of side hustle pay the beyond three years and I've contributed to a blog now and again for almost 10 years. Contributing to a blog is an ideal second job since you can chip away at it at whatever point you need, it tends to be done anyplace you have a web association, you don't need to work with anybody you would rather not work with, and it's not difficult to begin and stop at whatever point you need.

As I said before, I began Youthful Grown-up Cash in July 2012 determined to bring in sufficient cash to counterbalance our $1,000/month understudy loan installment. From that point forward, I've reached and outperformed that objective, and have met numerous different bloggers who have been fruitful at transforming writing for a blog into a second job. It tends to be finished.

There are a few disadvantages to writing for a blog. Some of the time I've alluded to writing for a blog as "the substance futile daily existence" since there are such countless sites out there putting out comparative substance. It's a steady fight to offer some incentive and get individuals to your site. It can require 6 a year of difficult work getting your blog laid out before you bring in any cash from it. In spite of the disadvantages, in the event that you are sufficiently committed, you have a decent possibility making part time job cash through your blog.

Publishing content to a blog accompanies a great deal of potential gain, which is the reason I think it makes for a decent second job. A companion of dig was on ESPN for a board about a Day to day Dream Sports outrage since he was recognized as a specialist because of his Day to day Dream Sports blog. No one can really tell where writing for a blog will take you.

SELLING ON ETSY

Etsy is an internet business commercial center where individuals can trade high quality or rare things and supplies. Etsy permits one of a kind produced merchandise as long as they fall under what they characterize as "remarkable, ", for example, using a slice and-sew shop to make garments you've planned.

In fact, selling on Etsy isn't possible from anyplace since it would be illogical and cost restrictive to send your items from, say, the Philippines, however it very well may be finished from the solace of your home.

Many individuals have constructed fruitful second jobs from Etsy. One model is Joan Olson and Aina Carr, who began the Etsy business Welkin on Air that spends significant time in special wedding shoes and other wedding-related things. They have almost 9,000 deals as of this composition.

One thing to remember with Etsy is that deals can begin slow. It took Joan and Aina two years before they began to get fair pay from their shop, yet that was essentially on the grounds that they re-contributed their profit.

At the point when I conversed with Joan, she focused on the need to have items that put your shop aside. In the most natural sounding way for her, "I think ordinarily individuals attempt to sell items that are now oversaturated on Etsy. On the off chance that there are now a few shops selling items like yours and you can't separate your item from theirs, you will wind up with an excessive amount of rivalry. In the event that your thing looks basically the same as another person's, multiple occasions a client will pick the less expensive thing."

VIRTUAL HELPER

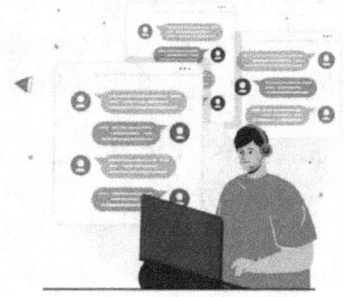

Remote helpers do a wide range of work for entrepreneurs. From noting messages to monitoring and handling financials, there is a considerable rundown of things that a menial helper can do.

In the event that you are seeming to be a menial helper as a feature of a part time job, you'll need to find an entrepreneur who will permit you to place in hours beyond the conventional 9-5 working day. While some might maintain that their remote helper should answer messages over the course of the day, others will be adaptable and permit you to finish fill in as have opportunity and energy.

One thing to remember whether you need to turn into a menial helper is that there are modest choices abroad for remote helpers. A few remote helpers will work all day for just $500 every month. Considering that, make certain to bring up how you separate yourself from an abroad remote helper, maybe by guiding out your capacity toward take on more significant level assignments, capacity to work with less course, the way that English is your most memorable language, and so on.

SOCIAL MEDIA MANAGEMENT

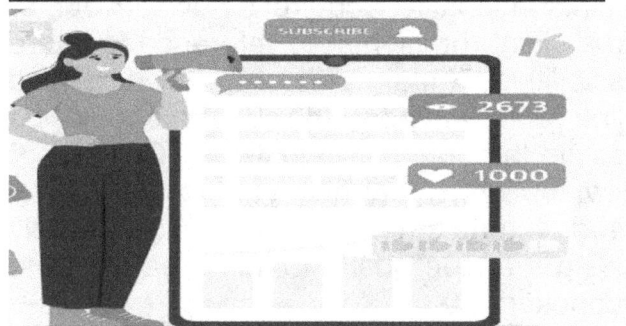

Online entertainment the executives is a help numerous remote helpers offer, yet it can likewise be an independent help offering. Certain individuals significantly offer administration of a particular virtual entertainment channel, as Pinterest.

There is a hustle antic requirement for powerful virtual entertainment the executives among brands and private ventures. Numerous organizations have either not focused via web-based entertainment or don't oversee it ideally. A few brands essentially despise running online entertainment so they do the absolute minimum. If somebody somehow happened to offer them virtual entertainment the board for a sensible expense there is a decent opportunity they'd take them up on it.

To begin in web-based entertainment the

board it's a good idea to offer free administrations to acquire a few encounter and a client (or clients) to reference to future possibilities. A main part of the work behind online entertainment the board should be possible through instruments like Cushion or Tailwind, which permits you to plan web-based entertainment postings, successfully making it a side hustle that is area free and not booked.

FLIPPING THINGS ON EBAY OR CRAIGSLIST

Flipping things on eBay or Craigslist is another "on the web" part time job that can be worthwhile for somebody who is great at spotting arrangements and preferences managing actual items rather than something altogether virtual.

There are various bloggers I realize who have discussed flipping things on eBay and Craigslist. It works like this: first, you track down something for inexpensively free at a carport deal, secondhand shop, or out and about. You fix it up or restore it, and afterward show it available to be purchased on Craigslist or eBay.

Simple straightforward?

Certain individuals take this to a higher level

and attempt to make a full-time pay out of it. One of my parent's neighbors resurfaces furniture as an everyday work. She is continually trading furniture and has culminated the specialty with a framework that works for her.

GRAPHIC DRAWING (DESIGN)

Visual computerization should be possible altogether on the web and opens up the way to numerous potential clients paying little heed to where they are found.

With for all intents and purposes each and every organization being available on the web, there is enormous interest for visual depiction work. Each private venture needs incredible marking and extraordinary plan, also the endless average size and huge organizations. Organizations likewise are continually rebranding, making a consistent, ceaseless stream of requests.

I conversed with Amanda Wahlund, who is currently a full-time independent visual originator, about her experience doing visual communication as a second job. Free work is an effective method for building a portfolio while likewise getting openness and building an organization of expected clients. Furthermore, she wishes she had invested more energy developing her second job business prior to turning into a full-time specialist. Getting an incredible site and getting a bigger base of paying clients are two different ways that can be achieved.

There is a ton of contest for visual depiction because of locales like Elance. I posted a task for another logo for Youthful Grown-up Cash and got 27 proposals in 24 hours or less. Indeed, that's what even considering, individuals will quite often favor employing project workers who were alluded to them. In the event that you can begin with a couple of clients furthermore, fabricate a strong standing, you will continuously have a developing number of possible clients.

CREDIT CARD STIRRING

Credit card stirring/churning is the method involved with pursuing Visas to get a sign-up reward and afterward hence shutting the cards whenever you have utilized the reward. It's a way a many individuals travel for inexpensively free. I consider it a second job since you are "making" cash during the time spent joining and shutting cards.

To give you a model, there was a Credit card that offered a $400 travel credit that can be utilized on any movement cost as long as you pursued the card and charged no less than $3,000 on it in 3 months or less. It has a yearly expense, however it's deferred for the main year. So in the event that you shift however much of your spending as could be expected to the card and hit the $3,000 required spending, you get the $400 credit. Different cards offer miles or even money back.

It's a given that you ought to possibly stir Visas on the off chance that you have no Credit card obligation, can completely take care of your Visa charge every month, and don't spend pointlessly to get the Credit card rewards. Prior to beginning, you ought to likewise investigate what oftentimes shutting cards will mean for your credit both in the short-and long haul.

OPINION-GIVER (PROVIDER)

Finishing up reviews is one of the most established ways of bringing in cash on the web, and advertisers' craving to hear shopper's thoughts on future items hasn't dialed back by any means.

One admonition I would give assuming that you choose to seek after this as a second job is that there are a ton of malicious locales out there that truly do not merit your time. A couple of the more real locales are:

- UserTesting
- 20/20 Board
- Harris Survey
- Nielsen Computerized Voice

One thing to be clear about is that you won't make a lot of cash finishing up studies or offering your perspective. This can be a decent side hustle to couple with opposite side hustles, similar to mystery shopping or even a seasonal work.

PODCASTING

Like contributing to a blog, podcasting can be a worthwhile area free part time job. There are various individuals who make a parttime or full-time living through podcasting. Assuming you can lay out a digital broadcast and fabricate a sizeable crowd, there will more likely than not be promoters in your specialty that will support episodes.

Like how independent composition or contributing to a blog can prompt new open doors, podcasting can prompt new open doors or even another profession. Podcasters have insight in sound creation as well as in building a crowd of people. They are somewhat sure things for organizations hoping to recruit or agreement out media creation.

There are several motivations behind why

individuals come up short at making a second job out of podcasting. In the first place, individuals battle getting those vital first audience members. It's more straightforward to showcase a digital broadcast in the event that there is as of now a blog or some kind of online entertainment presence laid out. Second, individuals appear to stop too soon. Webcasts are like web journals - they consume a large chunk of the day to lay out. Stopping after three, four, even ten digital recordings is by all accounts genuinely normal in the podcasting local area.

MAKING YOUTUBE VIDEOS

YouTube has been around for some time now and you probably have heard gossipy tidbits about individuals that make millions a year making YouTube recordings. While YouTube doesn't deliver how much unambiguous YouTube channels create, it's well realized that there are YouTubers who make in overabundance of $100k a year off of publicizing income.

I'm desirous of anybody who can create great video content. I'm not gifted nearby, but rather I in all actuality do believe it's the most worthwhile media road to seek after. As of late, organizations like Facebook have been moving into the video space and video makers can use the opposition for better publicizing rates.

Other than distributing YouTube recordings and bringing in cash off of publicizing, there are additionally many individuals (such as myself) who might like video content for their site/image/organization yet don't have what it takes to do as such. In the event that you can make quality recordings on YouTube, you quickly have an arrangement of your work, making it more probable that you will be recruited for independent work. In the event that you have video abilities and a few thoughts for a YouTube channel, it's an extraordinary way to seek after for side pay, particularly because of the possible potential gain of agreement video work.

CHAPTER 6

SMALL BUSINESS SIDE HUSTLES

There are many reasons somebody would need to zero in on a second job that can possibly transform into a full-time business. Maybe they would rather not stay in their present place of employment/vocation for eternity. Or on the other hand perhaps they like bringing in a lot of cash as an afterthought to make exiting the workforce a chance.

Anything that the reasons, there are many second jobs that can possibly transform into a full-time business. As a matter of fact, a considerable lot of the second jobs I've proactively referenced, like beginning a Simple business or a blog, can possibly develop into a full-time business.

In this segment, I need to get down on a couple of thoughts and methodologies for individuals explicitly hoping to begin a side hustle that can develop into a full-time business. Once more, remember that there is some cross-over with different segments, as these are by all accounts not the only side hustles that can possibly transform into a bigger business.

CREATING AN ONLINE PRODUCT TO SELL

Assuming you're searching for aloof web-based pay, there could be no more excellent method for doing it than to make a web-based item to sell. It requires none of the coordination of creation and conveyance that accompanies an actual item, and it can in a real sense make you cash while you rest.

One of the previous scholars for Youthful Grown-up Cash, jewel Alford, made an instructional class for individuals hoping to bring in cash as an independent essayist. While Feline has a ton of interest for her composing administrations, this was a brilliant move for her in light of the fact that any cash she makes off the course 6 is uninvolved. She doesn't need to work x hours or produce x posts for a site proprietor.

The course is made and individuals are buying and utilizing it with practically no extra time responsibility on her part.

Another incredible model is a Adroit Calculation sheet. I as of late bought a bookkeeping sheet on the site and cherished the framework that Janet set up. She can make recurring, automated revenue endlessly off of calculation sheets she has previously made. The deals and conveyance process is on the web and completely computerized.

Assuming you really want cash right away, this may not be the most ideal course for you. Yet, assuming you are OK monetarily and can sink a period into creating something to sell, this could be a savvy method for going for the basic reality that you have a shot at making a genuinely automated source of income.

CREATING A PHYSICAL PRODUCT TO MANUFACTURE AND SELL

One book that has had an enduring impact on me is Timothy Ferriss' The 4-Hour Long week of work. In the book he discusses "muses" which are basically organizations in light of an item that you make. The way in to an effective dream is making a framework where you reevaluate each feature of it, from assembling, to arrange satisfaction, to client care. This permits you to eliminate yourself as a proprietor and make uninvolved pay.

While I will more often than not favor online items that don't need fabricating, stock administration, or whatever else that accompanies an actual item, actual items really do enjoy a major benefit. They regularly are difficult to imitate and there are undeniably a bigger number of hindrances to section than organizations that are dependent on "virtual" items. There additionally are many organizations that can take on different parts of the production network and conveyance process, permitting the proprietor to eliminate themselves and money checks.

An illustration of an item that fits this portrayal is EarPeace.
Jay Clark made EarPeace and it plans to take care of the issue of ugly hearing assurance. Per Clark,
"EarPeace is high devotion hearing security that cuts back the volume without misshaping the sound, it's essentially imperceptible, agreeable, reusable, and comes in awesome bundling."

Another model is Square 36, a larger than usual yoga mat that Bounce Maydonik made with a colleague. It takes care of the issue of standard yoga mats being excessively little and deficient for exercise programs like P90X.

Both of these business people source their items from producers they found on Alibaba, and are phenomenal instances of actual items that are one of a kind and have a ton of potential gain. Not in the least does selling an actual item offer the potential for reliable, material, month to month pay, yet it likewise might possibly be offered not too far off to an external financial backer.

LAUNCHING A WEB-BASED SERVICE

Many electronic administrations have transformed into billion-dollar organizations. This is where you will track down the Facebook, Spotifys, and Ubers of the world. These administrations set aside individuals time and cash, as well as interface individuals.

Some online administrations are direct. For instance, eBay is a commercial center to trade products. Basic idea; confounded to execute. However, few out of every odd online help should be a billion-dollar thought. Curiously, most billion-dollar thoughts don't appear to be that convoluted (for example Airbnb's plan of action: coordinate momentary room, loft, and house rentals).

Online administrations don't need to a hustle antic embrace. You could begin an electronic help that is just a sole ownership that in the end develops into something greater. Some satisfied composing administrations began as one essayist and developed into business where tens or many journalists were welcomed on to take on work. The equivalent can be said about some tech counseling organizations that began as little organizations with a couple of workers yet in the long run developed into a lot greater organizations.

One illustration of a help based web-based business is Succeed Downpour Principal. Jen Portland began Succeed Downpour Man to assist individuals and organizations with their Succeed related issues. She fostered her abilities at her everyday work and saw the possibility to use her abilities to give Succeed administrations to other people. She presently runs Succeed Downpour Man full-time and has various subcontractors that she designates work to.

Jen's story delineates a significant point: assuming that there is a specific expertise that you have that is popular in your work environment, there is a decent opportunity that others and organizations have interest for that expertise too.

WEDDING-RELATED PRODUCTS AND SERVICES

One industry that I believe is great for second jobs is weddings. Weddings quite often occur around evening time or potentially toward the end of the week. Numerous merchants are required for each wedding, from music to taking special care of flower vendors. There is likewise a lot of cash in weddings and no indication of that pattern dialing back.

Since there is such a lot of interest in the wedding business, there is likewise the potential for some random wedding side hustle to transform into a full-time business. A couple of wedding second jobs that could transform into full-time organizations are:

RENTALS

Seats, beautifications, cloths, photograph booths...you name it, there is a business opportunity for it.

PHOTOGRAPHY
Customary photography, yet additionally "photograph stall" type photography.

COORDINATION
An ever increasing number of weddings are having "day of" facilitators that ensure everything moves along as expected. This could likewise incorporate wedding arranging.

MUSIC
From DJ administrations to unrecorded music, both at the service and gathering.

OFFICIANT
In the event that you appreciate public talking and weddings, you can make two or three hundred bucks for each wedding you direct.

WEDDING-RELATED CLOTHING
Recall the business I referenced in the Etsy area? They constructed a full-time business out of wedding shoes.

ENRICHMENTS
These can be uniquely designed

enhancements or gifts made explicitly for a given wedding, both for buy and lease. There are many individuals who get by as wedding sellers. There is no restriction to what these part time jobs can develop into, particularly for an innovative and business-disapproved of person. Indeed, even DJ administrations might appear to be a small time show, however our wedding DJ has fabricated a whole business out of it and presently has various representatives working for and addressing his image.

ACCOUNTING & TAX SERVICES

Most sole ownerships or even independent ventures basically can't legitimize a full-time bookkeeper. This opens up a chance for the people who work in Accounting or expense full-time, as these organizations are probably going to be more able to recruit somebody who are just accessible on evenings and ends of the week. In the event that you appreciate following funds and keeping monetary records, it very well may be a rewarding part time job.

I've worked all day as both a bookkeeper and monetary expert, however even I experience issues staying aware of the funds for my blog. Because of charges it's anything but a choice to not follow my income and costs, so it is possible that I need to accomplish the work or I need to reevaluate it. Each and every other entrepreneur is experiencing the same thing. There are certain individuals who focus on a particular specialty, for example, bloggers or Etsy storekeepers, and monitor their funds for them.

Charge administrations are not restricted to organizations, however, as there are many individuals who enlist CPAs to finish up their tax documents for them. I know various individuals who do this as a side hustle during the bustling duty season. It's a somewhat maintainable side hustle, as well, as there is a brief timeframe where it is incredibly bustling followed by numerous long periods of next to zero work.

CHAPTER 7

SELF-EMPLOYMENT SIDE HUSTLES

There are many individuals out there who are miserable in their positions and professions. They would rather not do it for eternity. They disdain the drive, they loathe having little command over their timetable, and they need to work for themselves.

It tends to be exceptionally dangerous to stop a steady regular task to seek after your fantasies. Particularly in the present monetary environment where most understudies graduate with lots of obligation, it's essentially impossible for some.

Fortunately it's within the realm of possibilities to begin a side that will ultimately transform into an independently employed vocation.

One of the potential gains to side hustling is the potential for becoming independently employed or a "solopreneur" as a like to call it.

Here are a few thoughts for second jobs that

give that potential gain.

SOVEREIGN/FREELANCE WRITING

Almost everybody knows how to compose articles or blog entries (or can figure out how to), and there is by all accounts a perpetual interest for new satisfied. This makes outsourcing a decent second job beginning stage.

I've utilized various independent scholars for Youthful Grown-up Cash throughout the long term and a couple of them are independent essayists full-time. What I've seen is that most independent authors battle to begin however whenever they are laid out it becomes simpler to land positions and charge more each hour.

So how would you begin in independent composition? It assists with having a site or blog that features your composition. When you have a site or blog, contact different websites/content destinations in your specialty. Inquire as to whether they are hoping to employ essayists and, on the off chance that not, propose to compose a free visitor post. This will assist you with getting your initial not many independent hustles and you can work from that point.

It's vital to not charge a lot from the get go. Indeed, composing for $10 or $20 a post doesn't sound attractive, however you can gradually increment.

WEB ENHANCEMENT

There is immense interest for web engineers. Enormous organizations need them, medium-sized organizations need them, little organizations need them and, surprisingly, sole owners need them.

Interest for web engineers won't dial back in light of the fact that the quantity of brands, organizations, and people who are searching for a positive web presence is continually expanding. On the off chance that you are great at web improvement, you will actually want to track down clients. When you have a strong portfolio and references to back you up, anything is possible.

Web improvement is something that functions admirably as a side hustle. You can burn through 5, 10, or 30 hours seven days dealing with it. When you have sufficient interest, you can raise costs and be fussy about which clients you work with and the amount you charge.

Over the recent years, I've had an extremely challenging time finding a quality Word Press website specialist. Pretty much every other blogger I've conversed with has battled to find an originator they were completely content with. I think this shows quality creators, as well as the interest that is out there for web advancement abilities could fill the void that exists that.

DATABASE COUNSELING

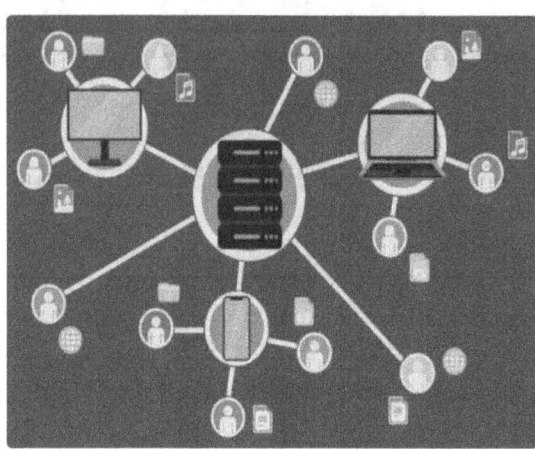

With the hustleantic measure of information that is accessible today, organizations are battling to keep up on the information the executives and information investigation front. While huge partnerships have a large number of dollars to toss at information the board, there are numerous little and fair size organizations that battle with finding reasonable answers for their information needs.

Data set counseling could be the best second job for you assuming that you invest impressive energy working with information in your regular work. You might have to invest more energy learning progressed data set ideas. The last thing you believe should do is recommend an answer for a client that doesn't work out as a result of your need of ability or aptitude.

It probably checks out to do some free or low-remuneration work for philanthropies or private companies. Philanthropies and private companies are probably going to be battling on this front, as most settled specialists and workers for hire charge a generally high for each hour rate. You can involve those first positions as references for future hustles, also that the proprietors or pioneers you worked with may begin alluding other entrepreneurs your way.

PROGRAMMING

Developers are in similarly appeal today and will keep on being for years to come. Innovation is being embedded into each aspect of our lives, and the pattern is probably going to proceed. This pattern addresses an immense chance for individuals with coding abilities.

Part time job occupations are easy to find for a companion of mine who is a developer. He's dealt with a Day to day Dream Sports (DFS) site where he was offered value as a trade off for his work as well as a paid hustle for a site that helps fill seats on personal luxury planes that sounds sitting unfilled.

For the personal luxury plane site, the code was at first moved to software engineers abroad, however my companion was acquired to tidy up the code and do a portion of the further developed coding.

One region inside programming that might be great for software engineers to zero in on is application improvement. Practically every organization needs an application. There is likewise a ton of chance for application designers to make their own applications that get income or on the other hand that they can offer to organizations.

PHOTOGRAPHY & FILMMAKING

Do you like taking pictures? Photography might be the side hustle for you. I have various companions and colleagues that have gone from doing photography as a side hustle to maintaining a photography business full-time.

The explanation photography is a particularly incredible side hustle is on the grounds that there is a ton of interest for photography on evenings and ends of the week. Families who need photos ordinarily need to plan the shoot beyond their 9-5 positions. Weddings are quite often toward the end of the week. Different occasions, similar to shows or games, regularly happen at night.

However, photography has its disadvantages. On the off chance that you are hoping to transform it into a regular work, you should proceed with the night and end of the week work plan even in the wake of making the change to everyday work, which isn't beneficial all of the time. Furthermore, there is a great deal of rivalry here, particularly as cameras and innovation make it a lot more straightforward for even untalented photographic artists to take "great" pictures.

So, there is for all intents and purposes limitless interest for picture takers. Individuals will keep on getting hitched and need photographic artists, occasions will keep on being booked where picture takers are required, and families will keep on craving family photograph shoots. It's not difficult to gradually develop a huge second job photography business and afterward do the change to everyday work, whenever wanted.

Photography is, by and large, reference based. This makes it crucial for not cheat while initially beginning in the photography business. It might try and check out to accomplish some work for nothing until you have developed an arrangement of models for future clients. It's a given that having a site and web-based entertainment presence will be key for roping in possible clients.

A large portion of the thing I said about photography can likewise be applied to videography. There is a ton of interest, particularly in the wedding business, for quality videographers. It's turning out to be to a greater extent a need rather than a "pleasant to-have" for organizations to create and exhibit video content attached to their image. Indeed "solopreneurs" and people are hoping to have recordings made to work on their image and put themselves aside from their opposition.

CHAPTER 8

LOCAL SIDE HUSTLES

One of my number one stories I like to share with respect to the "remote" versus "expected to be genuinely present" work banter includes a pipes issue I had at my home. I was working in bookkeeping at that point and had the option to work from a distance depending on the situation. The handyman was taking care of his responsibilities and inquired as to whether I was telecommuting. I said OK, and he said that should be truly good to have that choice.

While it is good to have the choice to work from anyplace, it additionally implies I rival a huge number of individuals that my handyman doesn't contend with. As a matter of fact, around the time handyman was finished, we were amidst a series of reevaluating and I went through endless hours preparing individuals from India.

The handyman, then again, will constantly have interest. Of course, he rivals other pipes organizations nearby, yet the opposition is substantially more restricted than going up against a huge number of individuals who can take care of your business abroad (for fundamentally less cash, I could add).

In this part, I need to address what I call "Local" or "neighborhood" side hustles. They are not side hustles that will be done on the web, nor are they side hustles that include being utilized by another person. Generally, they likewise miss the mark concerning having genuine capability of being a regular work yet I think this really makes them much more appealing for individuals searching for a second job.

DOGGISH WALKING

Is your everyday work beyond a normal 9-5 working day? Is it true or not that you are at home during the day? Above all, do you like pets?

In the event that you responded to yes to these inquiries, you should think about turning into a dog walker. As per Care.com, the typical compensation for a dog walker is $11.25/hour, however I've seen postings going from $10 to $30+ each 30-minute walk. You can join on Care.com to be a dog walker, as well as view work postings.

This is an ideal second job for somebody who loves dogs and has a timetable that doesn't adjust to a regular 9-5. The truth for the majority working experts is that they are gone longer than 8 hours per day. With both my significant other and I working ordinary 9-

5 positions, we so far have ruled against getting a dog, for the most part since we would not be able to let them out during the day. That choice might change not too far off assuming our pay increments and we can legitimize employing somebody to walk our dog on non-weekend days.

There are numerous families that have chosen to get a dog and are able to pay somebody to walk it around mid-afternoon, or even in the first part of the day or night.

PET OR/AND HOUSE SITTING

Anybody with a pet knows how troublesome it tends to be to track down somebody to deal with it when they leave town. In the event that you will deal with pets while individuals are away, you can put forth a pleasant side pay with negligible attempt. Because of the web, it's become progressively simple for animal people to track down individuals to deal with their pets, as well as the other way around. Sites like Rover.com, DogVacay.com, and Care.com are extraordinary spots to list your administrations, accessibility, and experience.

While not precisely logical correlation, I truly do figure pet consideration can measure up to independent writing as in you ought to charge less until you have a couple of positive surveys and some experience added to your repertoire. Audits and references are critical!

Short-term or childcare for pets can net you somewhere in the range of $20 to $100+ each evening. The potential for money will change contingent upon area, number and kind of pets, and different variables. Pet consideration can function admirably for individuals who work from home since it doesn't influence their 9-5 plan for getting work done.

CHILD CARE

As I referenced before, my better half kept on working at YMCA Kid's Stuff even in the wake of moving on from school. She would take Saturday shifts and just quit once she began graduate school. While she said it very well may be unpleasant when there are an excessive number of kids without a moment's delay, it was work she delighted in and was a decent wellspring of side pay.

While her work in kid care was at a business, there are open doors for those in their 20s and 30s to watch kids on evenings and ends of the week. There are two methodologies that can be taken while chasing after kid care as a part time job, each with upsides and downsides.

The first is to spread the word about your goals as broadly as could be expected. In any event, posting on Facebook that you are looking to keep an eye on the side could assist you with getting a couple of occupations. The reward in beginning with individuals you know is that you are reasonable currently acquainted with the messes with you will watch. When individuals know that you are hoping to bring in some cash as an afterthought through kid care, you will probably help some work through references. This could be a decent side hustle for guardians, as well, as you as of now are watching kids so having extra children to watch will not degrade your standard timetable.

The subsequent methodology is setting up a profile on a site prefer Care.com and getting drives as such. The advantage here isn't expecting to connect with individuals you know, which could be off-kilter in the event that you wind up watching your companions kids, since there is an opportunity they might consider it to be some help as opposed to something you ought to get installment for.

RENTING PLOT

In the event that you're hoping to differentiate your pay and have some additional room in your home or condo, it could seem OK to get a flat mate. Numerous school graduates feel like it's their "right" to live alone and that they deserve it. Yet, on the off chance that you're battling with educational loan obligation and have space that could be shared, it very well might be too huge of a monetary benefit to miss.

Other than having a room mate, one thing that current and future mortgage holders might need to consider is the chance of making a condo inside their home. There several things to remember whether you choose to go the space rental course. Continuously have a marked agreement set up. There is a ton of hazard in not having an agreement and agreements set assumptions for the two players. I likewise would prescribe being particular while picking who to impart your space to. You need to have shared trust and regard, so having somebody move in who you definitely realize will constantly be great.

One more way to deal with space leasing that is turning out to be ridiculously well known is Airbnb. Airbnb is a site where you can list excursion rentals as well as track down get-away rentals to book. As of this composition, there are more than 1.5 million postings in 34 thousand urban areas and 190 nations.

The amount you can cause will to differ contingent upon city and what you are leasing. A few rentals are the whole loft/house, while others are only a room or even a common room. Many individuals are seeking travel for inexpensively will take a sofa or shared room on the off chance that it implies they can set aside cash. In the event that you are happy with inviting others into your home and love being a host, this could turn out to be an extraordinary part time job for you.

DELIVERY DRIVER

While the greater part of conveyance drivers are utilized by an organization, there is more open door today than any other time for individuals to work as self employed entities and work on their own timetable.

Uber is by a wide margin the most popular "Delivery" administration, yet all the same it's not alone. There are numerous new businesses, for example, Deliv and SpoonRocket that are attempting to challenge the customary delivery model.

The unrest in the conveyance business will play for the people who are hoping to put in a couple of hours seven days conveying things as a part time job. It's a success for all interested parties, as individuals don't need to focus on being a representative and the organizations hoping to have things conveyed don't need to face the monetary gamble challenges full-time workers.

Assuming this side hustle sounds fascinating to you, check and check whether any of the conveyance new businesses work in your space and watch out for organizations that are venturing into new business sectors. The business sectors they serve might be restricted now, yet monster organizations like Uber were likewise in only a couple of business sectors at first.

TEACHING/INSTRUCTING

There will constantly be interest for coaches and instructors. Guardians believe that their children should find success, and assuming that implies paying somebody to help them in a space of battle, so be it.

In the event that you are bilingual, this can be an especially rewarding second job. Being able to communicate in more than one language is something that many guardians look for their kids, and commonly taking courses in school will not exactly give somebody enough openness to become familiar.

I had a companion who gave guitar examples all through school. He was charging in overabundance of $50/hour, and guardians were able to pay his rate. He did this as an everyday occupation during school, yet you can envision how simple it is keep on giving examples on evenings and ends of the week once he got a "standard" 9-5.

REFFING SPORTS

With how crazy youth sports has turned into (it's not difficult to be critical when you don't have children of your own), there is a hustleantic requirement for refs to direct the endless competitions and games that happen each and every seven day stretch of the year.

Likewise with most things, the amount you make will differ. Varsity and JV games will pay more than youth games. I've heard that secondary school football will pay around $50 a game and soccer around $35 a game. Once more, this will shift by city and state.

One thing to remember is that adolescent and varsity sports are not by any means the only socioeconomics that need refs. There are loads of grown-up associations that compensation to have refs. For instance, consider all the sluggish pitch softball associations that happen each mid year and fall.

In the event that you appreciate sports and figure you will actually want to manage guardians hollering at you, being a ref can be an extraordinary second job. One of my previous chief's better half refs secondary school football and, from my comprehension, does it because of unadulterated happiness the side pay is only a reward.

COACHING SPORTS

Like the interest for refs, there is a ton of interest for mentors. Some instructing positions are neglected, yet many really do repay mentors for their time and exertion.

Instructing can be a remunerating second job for various reasons. For some mentors, there is a fulfillment in forming individuals into better competitors and people. Instructing likewise permits previous competitors to remain associated with a game notwithstanding being past their playing days. At long last, many secondary school mentors get a payment for each season they mentor, making it an ideal transient part time job with a distinct beginning and end date.

A companion of mine mentors swimming at the YMCA once per week for 90 minutes. Besides the fact that she gets compensated a bit, however she likewise gets a free rec center enrollment for her loved ones. She additionally gets free kid care while she mentors. Not a terrible arrangement!

CLINICAL EXPLORATION STUDIES

Clinical exploration is a major field and, of course, those leading the examination need individuals to take part in the examination. There are normally consistently research concentrates on going on that repay individuals for their time, particularly on the off chance that you have different clinical sicknesses, like asthma, diabetes, and so on.

While I haven't searched out clinical exploration studies, I joined and meet all requirements for one connected with asthma and sensitivities. The projected remuneration is $900. The review hasn't begun at this point however I suspect it might turn out to be hard to take part in with an ordinary 9-5 work, except if they have adaptable hours.

I wouldn't suggest taking part in clinical exploration concentrates as an essential side hustle, yet it very well may be an effective method for bringing in some additional cash every once in a while, expecting you qualify.

MOVING SERVICES

With regards to part time jobs, the greater an issue you can tackle, the better. Moving is an enormous cerebral pain and an unpleasant time for a great many people. This presents a chance for individuals who will assist with making the experience somewhat less difficult.

Many individuals like to continue toward the end of the week, so the timing is ready for a side hustle. Moving administrations could be pretty much as basic as charging each hour that you help or as perplexing as giving a moving truck/gear and a little team to take the action effective.

Assuming that you're ready to lift more than the normal individual and wouldn't fret accomplishing some actual work each end of the week, moving administrations can be an incredible part time job. Increment your possibilities for progress by laying out a formal LLC, review agreements to shield yourself from potential harms caused all the while. The more expert you introduce yourself, the more quiet individuals to whom you offer your assistance will be.

CHAPTER 9

UPSIDE - THE UNEXPECTED GAINS

The main motivation I love part time jobs can be captured in single word: upside.

Second jobs have potential for colossal potential gain. Numerous organizations and second professions have begun as a part time job. One of my number one instances of part time jobs having hustle antic potential gain is the funny cartoon Dilbert. Many individuals don't have the foggiest idea about that Scott Adams, organizer behind Dilbert, wasn't generally an illustrator. Dilbert began as a second job while Adams worked a 9-5.

All that yet Win Enormous, he attempted many second jobs and organizations in his extra time before beginning Dilbert. They included, in addition to other things, making PC games, a web video organization, and a staple home conveyance administration. Practically all either fizzled or were deserted.

Through a blend of devotion, exertion, karma, and timing, Adams prevailed with regards to doing what most just fantasy about: transforming a side hustle into a business that makes a large number of dollars. The narrative of Dilbert is a rousing one for any individual who is thinking about checking side hustles out. Second jobs really can possibly completely change you.

Most side hustles won't transform into million-dollar organizations, yet some will. In any event, taking a temporary occupation as a second job has expected potential gain, as no one can really tell who you will meet or what thoughts you will be presented to simultaneously. Not to notice the way that being proactive about settling obligation will normally open up amazing open doors, since not having obligation unavoidably permits you to make the most of additional potential open doors.

This part is about the potential gain of having a second job. In the event that you're not currently roused to begin a part time job, you will be toward this section's end. On the off chance that you as of now are anticipating beginning a side hustle, you will acquire new viewpoints and thoughts of how you can best use a part time job to better different aspects of your life. At last, I will address what I like to call "high level part time job potential" which is utilizing a side hustle to begin another side hustle (it will seem OK, believe me).

THE BENEFIT OF CONNECTIONS

Having a second job will normally furnish you with associations that you in any case wouldn't have. These associations can prompt new (and better) positions, new clients, and new business bodies.

This is the most compelling motivation why I figure everybody ought to have a blog or specialty site about something they are keen on. A blog is an ideal part time job since it makes it extremely simple to meet individuals and organization. For instance, with individual accounting sites there is a whole yearly meeting devoted to individual budget bloggers. Numerous bloggers likewise remark on each other's posts, share articles, and overall will help one another.

While it might take some time before your blog develops sufficiently huge to draw in publicists, essentially having a blog will ultimately get an ordinary progression of brands and organizations who are keen on working with you. This can prompt open doors that in any case wouldn't be imaginable, like promoting
agreements, organizations, from there, the sky is the limit.

For my purposes, four open doors came

about exclusively from having a side hustle, and all the more explicitly, a blog. They are:

POSSIBLE STARTUP MONEY
As I referenced before, I used to work for a blog during school. I met the blog proprietor through my political blog. I've kept in contact with him and I presently representative

notice for the different sites he's gained throughout the long term. As of late I've referenced my longing to send off a business and he's communicated his advantage in possibly providing me with capital in return for value in the organization. Any individual who has attempted to send off a business or fund-raise for another business will let you know exactly the way in which significant an association like this is.

SPREEDSHEET SIDE HUSTLE
Recall Janet Kim, pioneer behind Canny Calculation sheets, who I referenced prior? I at first contacted her to check whether she was keen on having her business highlighted on my blog. As we began messaging to and fro, it ended up being clear there was potential for cooperation past Youthful Grown-up Cash. I currently have the valuable chance to distribute and sell my calculation sheets on her site and get a portion of the income they get. Hi aloof side

hustle pay!

FREE OUTING TO HAWAII
Prior, I referenced that entering giveaways was a side hustle of mine. What I didn't make reference to was the greatest award I at any point won: an excursion to Hawaii.

I won the excursion through a reference rivalry that the organization IZEA put on. IZEA had another stage for facilitating web-based entertainment notices and believed more individuals should pursue it. I wound up alluding the a great many people during the fourteen day time frame the challenge ran for and won the Hawaii trip.

In the event that I hadn't begun a blog, I couldn't have ever fabricated the crowd or organization important to get the references expected to win the opposition.

THIS BOOK
If not for my blog, I couldn't have ever had the chance to compose this book, or possibly could never have had the chance to collaborate with a fantastic distributer like Mango. My recommendation to individuals who have an objective of distributing a book is equivalent to my guidance for those hoping to break into independent composition: begin a blog.

While I principally centered around my contributing to a blog side hustle in this segment, I must bring up that this isn't the main side hustle that has had organizing benefits.

One of my opposite side hustles, calculation sheet counseling, prompted a proposal to be a Money Chief for a business I had talked with. While I eventually didn't take the work, it demonstrates that having a side hustle can rapidly prompt bids for employment what's more, new profession open doors.

What side hustles can offer you is this: the capacity to at the same time settle your obligation with your 9-5 pay while likewise assembling your business. I have numerous companions who have begun photography, independent composition, or another kind of side hustle that at last transformed into a regular work.

Beginning a business as a side hustle permits you to develop customers through an organization of clients, as well as lay out clients who will reliably allude you.

NEW ABILITIES THAT SUPPORT WITH YOUR 9-5

Having a side hustle can help you accomplish new or further developed abilities for your 9-5. That is one motivation behind why I believe it's ideal to find a side hustle that mixes something you appreciate doing with something that requires abilities that are adaptable to your everyday work.

It was from the beginning in my post-school profession that I took up bookkeeping sheet counseling as a side hustle. Since I was an bookkeeper at that point, you can envision that what I realized during my side hustle straightforwardly helped me in my 9-5. It likewise constrained me to investigate choices and recipes in a calculation sheet that I in any case could never have investigated.

A few abilities you gain during a side hustle aren't as adaptable, or if nothing else the worth of the expertise you created doesn't appear to work with your 9-5. That appeared to be the situation with publishing content to a blog, yet through contributing to a blog I've acquired better relationship building abilities and arranging abilities, as I generally need to examine and haggle with brand chiefs and entrepreneurs in the everyday administration of my blog.

One vital method for pondering your side hustle is by zeroing in on an expertise you really want to improve for your 9-5. On the off chance that you're a sorry extrovert or you loath public talking, you could foster those abilities by agreeing with on a particular stance hustle that compels you to work straightforwardly with individuals. It may not be agreeable from the get go, yet the decent thing about a side hustle is that you should just go for it; you can continuously stop and begin another one.

Getting compensated to foster abilities that will assist with your 9-5 is an incredible method for moving toward your side hustle. It could bring about getting more cash at your 9-5 and you can't beat getting compensated to foster your abilities.

FINANCIAL CERTAINTY

As somebody who has invested a ton of energy thinking, perusing, and expounding on individual accounting records, I think one thing is unquestionable: obligation prompts dread. The people who are agreeable monetarily have that base degree of dread eliminated and have "better" things to stress over, for example, achieving objectives in their profession or business, being in ideal wellbeing, making a timetable that considers most extreme time doing things they love, etc. On the off chance that you are battling with obligation, it's difficult to concentrate however much you'd like on those "next level" concerns.

Try not to misunderstand me, certain individuals who appear to be wealthy have significantly more obligation and feeling of dread toward funds than others, yet I'm centered around the trepidation that comes from living check to-check, having a boatload of obligation, or essentially not having positive expectations about your monetary circumstance.

I've been there. I have bunches of objectives throughout everyday life except couldn't start to zero in on those greater objectives when I have a lot of educational loan obligation looming over my head. Once in a while a 9-5 pay simply won't cut it. Indeed, even a "great" pay normally doesn't consider rapidly and definitely settling understudy loans.

This is where a side hustle gives you the one thing that might possibly change your life: financial confidence.

It's inconceivable the mental impact bringing in even a minimal expenditure outside of your 9-5 can have on your life. In any event, making $500 or $1,000 extra a month can give a monetary certainty that was unthinkable with simply your 9-5 pay. Part of that comes from the way that side hustle pay is something that you really want to proactively seek after; nobody compels you to seek after a side hustles.

Getting a tad of cash outside of your 9-5 powers you to understand that it's within the realm of possibilities to build your pay assuming you are sufficiently roused. Your 9-5 pay does not limit you. I

t is not necessarily the case that a 9-5 is something terrible. There are many individuals who work side hustles who have zero desire to stop there 9-5. A portion of those individuals even gets more cash-flow through their side hustle than their everyday work.

Regardless of whether you take care of all your obligation, there is as yet a hustle antic upside to having a side hustle. We'll talk about that next.

AFTER DEPT: HOW SIDE HUSTLES CAN LIFTOFF YOU AHEAD FINANCIALLY

It very well might be challenging to envision having no obligation, however assuming you are persuaded and inquisitive enough to peruse this book I'm sure that you will ultimately take care of all your dept. It may not be for one year, five years, or a decade, however you'll arrive.

In the event that you take care of your obligation utilizing side hustles, you enjoy an enormous upper hand over others. Since you've been using a subsequent revenue stream to take care of your obligation, when that obligation is gone, the optional revenue stream no longer goes towards obligation and on second thought begins to work in your financial balance. This makes it a lot more straightforward to excel in light of the fact that you have a whole "reward" revenue stream to use.

While you may not be as inspired to side hustle with obligation done looming over your head, excelling monetarily can act as another inspiration. Consider the effect that even an extra $1,000 a month can have on your funds.

Assuming you make $1,000 in side hustle pay consistently for the following 10 years and store it into a speculation account that makes 8% premium, with premium accumulated month to month, you will have roughly $184,000 toward the finish of the 10 years.

That is sufficient to purchase an investment property for cash that can be utilized as an automated revenue hotspot until the end of your life. Or on the other hand in the event that you purchased a stock like AT&T with roughly a 5.5% profit yield, you would have automated revenue of around $10,000 per year. On the off chance that you made $2,000 a month in side hustle pay during those 10 years, you'd have an astounding $368,000 to contribute, which brings about somewhat more than $20,000 a year in recurring, automated revenue (assuming you put resources into a stock with a profit yield of 5.5%).

Recollect this is all notwithstanding your full-time pay,
which is the reason side hustle pay is a particularly extraordinary method for excelling monetarily.

HIGH LEVEL SIDE HUSTLE POTENTIAL

One way that side hustles give upside is through what I like to call progressed side hustle potential. Prior I referenced the possibility of a side hustle that includes making, assembling, and selling a special item. This side hustle will commonly require huge number of dollars of cash front and center and just isn't possible for a great many people who are attempting to take care of obligation and construct a strong monetary base.

Consider this situation. You have been working your side hustle two or three years at this point. You have utilized your side hustle pay to balance your obligation installments, save a mystery stash, and have some cash left finished. The "extra" cash could be utilized to put resources into another side hustle, for example, the remarkable item side hustle, that you in any case wouldn't have the option to take on.

Utilizing side hustle pay to require on a subsequent side hustle is an extraordinary method for putting resources into something that you wouldn't involve your standard 9-5 pay for. It additionally permits you to face risk that you in any case wouldn't happy interpretation of.

One more illustration of a high level side hustle procedure is using your most memorable side hustle to scale your business. A few fruitful bloggers scale their side hustle by beginning or buying extra sites. This takes into account using a similar asset pool across different web journals. For instance, rather than employing an essayist for your webpage, you can enlist an author to compose across three distinct sites.

Side hustles might appear to be a drudgery, particularly in the event that you pick one that pays nothing from the get go. In any event, when you are bringing in cash, it tends to be depleting investing your extra energy working. Zeroing in on the possible upside, as well as the unavoidable monetary advantages of side hustles, can assist you with remaining propelled in any event, when you would rather not hustle. Keep your eyes open for chances to use your side hustle and consistently recall why you began side hustling in any case.

In thousands $

year	Year deposit	Yea Interest	Total Deposits	Total Interest	Balance
1	$0	$1	$12	$1	$13
2	$12	$2	$24	$2	$26
3	$12	$3	$36	$5	$41
4	$12	$4	$48	$9	$77
5	$12	$5	$60	$14	$74
6	$12	$7	$72	$21	$93
7	$12	$8	$84	$29	$113
8	$12	$10	$96	$39	$135
9	$12	$12	$108	$50	$158
10	$12	$14	$120	$64	$184

CHAPTER 10

SIDE HUSTLE HACKS

Second jobs can be energizing temporarily however can rapidly begin feeling like a weight, making them hard to keep up with. It's not difficult to second job when your inspiration is high, however what might be said about a year in when you simply need a break? For sure on the off chance that you become ill of the work as you compose your 500th blog entry, or answer your 3,000th email? When will it stop?

Side hustling can be challenging to coordinate into your life, yet for the majority individuals the advantages of second jobs offset the negatives, so they stay with it. In the event that you are sufficiently proactive to begin a part time job in any case, you obviously have the drive to tackle issues by making a move as opposed to pausing for a minute and harping on your mishap.

This section is about how to second job better. All things considered, on the off chance that you can side hustle better, for what reason couldn't you? It very well may be the contrast between dealing with your part time job 20 hours per week as opposed to chipping away at it 10 hours per week, or the distinction between having the option to shuffle all that as opposed to reaching a stopping point also, wearing out.

We should start it off by discussing the abilities to zero in on the off chance that you need to find actual success at second jobs.

SKILLS TO FOCUS ON FOR N SUCCESSFUL SIDE HUSTLE

Other than being roused by a monetary objective, I think there are a couple of explicit abilities that assist individuals with succeeding when they part time job. The following are 5 abilities that I suggest individuals center around improving if they have any desire to coordinate side hustling into their life effectively:

TIME MANAGEMENT
Prior in the book I discussed assessing whether you have the limit with regards to a side hustle. It's difficult to squeeze a side hustle into a generally pressed plan, however it is conceivable. It most likely isn't is business as usual that the people who can effectively second job are perfect at using time effectively.

Beginning and staying with a second job will be undeniably challenging in the event that you're not in that frame of mind of arranging your time. Getting better at using time productively can be essentially as straightforward as adhering to a schedule and saying "no" to things

On the off chance that you don't at present

utilize a schedule application like Viewpoint or Google Schedule, you will need to get everything rolling quickly. Indeed, that incorporates arranging out your nights and ends of the week. You really want to save blocks of time for your second job, and for all the other things, if you need to find success. One justification for why part time jobs like tending to tables or conveying food are some of the time simpler than additional adaptable side hustles is on the grounds that you are compelled to adhere to a timetable.

APTITUDE TO PRIORITIZE
Having the option to focus on is one more fundamental ability for any effective side hawker. Having a second job implies you have restricted spare energy, since some (or most) is being eaten up close by hustle. So in your restricted extra energy, would you say you are ready to single out what's significant enough for your time and consideration? Said in an unexpected way, would you say you are ready to allow the immaterial things to go unaddressed?

It's not difficult to attempt to "do everything, " except it's not feasible. All on an ordinary end of the week, you won't have the option to figure out multiple times, clean your entire house, manage life's liabilities, get 8 hours of rest an evening, invest a lot of energy with loved ones, and work 12 hours on your second job. Something's need to give! This is where singling out needs matter. On the off chance that your side hustle isn't really important, you won't stay with it long haul.

On the off chance that you have a side hustle where you can work on some random undertaking on a long plan for the day, it turns out to be significantly more critical to conclude what is important and what doesn't. Any individual who has begun a blog realizes you could burn through day in and day out getting things done to work on your webpage, yet actually 20% of the work will give 80% of the outcomes. Having the option to perceive this and completely finish just zeroing in on the thing matters is something that everybody can get better at.

CAPACITY TO CORRECT AND CHANGING CIRCUMSTANCES
On one occasion I received an email around 9AM from a promoter saying they would repay me $150 in the event that I distributed a survey of a brief narrative. There was a trick: the survey must be up by 2PM. Furthermore, this was on a work day.

Rather than allowing the chance to pass, I contacted a companion who had made the progress to a full-time independent essayist.

She had the option to compose the survey and get it distributed with maybe some time to spare, and everybody included benefited.

Having the option to adjust to changing circumstances is a basic expertise for individuals who second job. It's a piece unexpected that this expertise is in a similar rundown as "using time productively, " however they truly can cooperate. In the event that a period delicate open door comes your direction, would you say you are ready to deal with your chance to make it work? Or on the other hand will you pass up a major opportunity since you mightn't?

FOCUS ON THE MAIN CONCERN
You don't need to be a bookkeeper to realize that zeroing in on the main concern is significant in any work or business. The main concern is how much cash that will ultimately go into your financial balance, so it should be a tremendous focal point of your second job.

How might you get better at "zeroing in on the main concern?" By reliably assessing whether what you are doing is the best utilization of your time for how much cash you are getting compensated. For certain individuals, taking on a temporary occupation as a part time job checks out in light of the fact that they need cash pronto.

For other people, it could seem OK to search out a part time job that has potential for higher $/hour, however isn't really predictable, basically not before all else.

This ties into having the option to really focus on. While it very well may be questionable for certain second jobs, it's critical to basically ask yourself "how is this influencing my main concern?" You might find that a portion of the things you have on your plan for the day truly won't influence your primary concern and are more probable only "good to have." Time is excessively valuable with a side hustle: drop those unrewarding errands!

SPECIFIED//TECHNICAL SKILLS
Having specialized abilities isn't generally fundamental for doing great in a second job, yet for specific side hustles it tends to be an immense assistance. On the off chance that you are beginning a part time job that expects you to learn and use different programming programs, it's fundamental that you have essentially fundamental specialized abilities. On the off chance that it takes you days or weeks to become familiar with a product program that is crucial for your business, you will battle basically on the grounds that side hustles drive you to work on a more limited timetable.

On the off chance that you're not educated or despise dealing with PCs, don't seek after a part time job that is reliant upon your specialized abilities. You will probably wear out from the long periods of preparing that will be expected to keep up. You'll be in an ideal situation seeking after something that plays more to your assets.

These are a couple of the abilities that I figure individuals ought to zero in on to prevail in side hustles. Keep in mind, time is valuable with regards to side hustles. You are consequently restricted by the way that you are attempting to seek after something on top of an everyday work.

ONLINE DEVICES THAT ASSIST WITH SIDE HUSTLES

There are in a real sense many applications that can assist you with running a second job better. I'll share a not many that I have viewed as valuable. These will be more material to individuals running an internet based side hustle however there are some applications that are pertinent to basically any side hustle.

GOOGLE CALENDAR
It's a lot more straightforward to adhere to a schedule when you can refresh it from your telephone. Google Schedule is the ideal schedule application since you can refresh it in a hurry and it synchronizes between your PC and telephone. I utilize my Google Schedule strictly.

GOOGLE DRIVE
I consider Google Drive as serving a comparative capability as Microsoft Office, yet cloud-based. There is a word handling application (Google Docs), an accounting sheet application (Google Sheets), and a PowerPoint-like application (Google Slides).

The greatest advantage of Google Drive is that different individuals can be in a record simultaneously and everybody can alter at the same time. Likewise, altering and sharing is essentially as straightforward as going to the URL related with the archive or bookkeeping sheet.

I have a publication schedule for my blog where my scholars can see what subject I have planned for them on which day, as well as make alters to the actual schedule. I've involved Google Docs in the past to post employment opportunities.

DROPBOX
Dropbox is a distributed storage application that is allowed to utilize something like a specific measure of extra room. This has been a lifeline when I have a huge document to impart to somebody and I can't email it to them. As a matter of fact, I would contend that it's significantly simpler and more commonsense to share records through Dropbox than over email.

MICROSOFT OUTLOOK
Indeed, we as a whole realize email is helpful, so for what reason am I getting down on Microsoft Standpoint? Microsoft Standpoint is simpler to use than online applications like Gmail and has more choices and usefulness. It was a couple of years prior that I originally synchronized my

Gmail and site email to Viewpoint and it's been a lifeline from an efficiency and effectiveness stance.

BUFFER

In the event that you are dynamic via virtual entertainment, Cushion is a fundamental application. With Support you can plan virtual entertainment posts on Twitter and Facebook. You can plan for explicit times or you can decide to place posts in your line that will be posted at set times every day. Estimating begins at $10/month or $102/year.

TAILWIND

Tailwind is like Cushion however is made for Pinterest. You can plan pins and view examination that let you know the best opportunity to stick. It costs $10/month to utilize Tailwind.

GUMROAD

Gumroad is a site that makes it simple to sell virtual items on the web. Many individuals sell courses, digital books, music, and more through the Gumroad site. There is an exchange expense of $0.25 for every deal as well as a 5% charge for each sold item. There are no month to month expenses. Gumroad permits venders to zero in on their items as opposed to dealing with a deal and conveyance framework, and makes it simple to acknowledge for all intents and purposes any kind of installment.

PAYPAL

As a web-based side-trickster, I depend on PayPal. I've involved it consistently for over three years now and it's indisputably the simplest method for sending and get installments. While there are exchange charges, it normally has been worth the effort taking into account how simple and all inclusive PayPal is.

> *"These are only a couple of instances of uses that will make your life simpler as a side hawker. There are lots of other applications that you might view as helpful as you attempt to coordinate and smooth out your part time job, yet these are the ones that I would enthusiastically suggest looking at".*

TIME HACKS FOR SIDE HUSTLES

Not to continue on pointlessly, but rather time is significant with side hustles. Tracking down ways of making additional opportunity for yourself is critical.

Notwithstanding what second job you have, there are a couple of things you can do to save time.

AVOID RUSH HOUR
Do you have 60 minutes in addition to drive to work because of busy time? In the event that you can't move your work hours around, consider going to the library or a bistro after work and dealing with your plan for the day for a little while. Not exclusively will you finish a ton yet you'll likewise chop your drive time somewhere near 1/2 or even 1/3 of what it would be.

RECRUIT HELP AROUND YOUR HOME
Need to have some spare energy, yet additionally need to side hustle? You might have to rethink some work around your home. This could mean having somebody confessed all one time per week or paying somebody to trim your grass. It could likewise mean employing out work as opposed to going the DIY course. Keep in mind, however, that to legitimize

reevaluating you want to make more each hour than you are paying the individual you are
moving to.

FIND SURPRISING TIMES TO WORK

Early mornings. A 5-minute break. Noon. 30 minutes prior to hitting the hay. While you are on a treadmill. Find those dark times where you can rapidly put out some work and you will be astonished exactly the amount you can get done during time that in any case would have been spent doing useless things.

CONCENTRATION AND FIXATION

Online side hustles are the most horrendously terrible with regards to interruptions and zeroing in on the job that needs to be done can be troublesome. In the event that you're at home dealing with your PC, there will constantly be 100 interruptions. In the event that you center during work time, you could wind up cutting how much time you spend on your second job while obtain similar outcomes from an efficiency and monetary viewpoint. Limit interruptions whenever the situation allows.

Utilizing these hacks to all the more likely use your time will bring about not so much pressure but rather more available energy.

Quit perusing Facebook and Twitter when you ought to be chipping away at things that really offer some incentive!

SECOND JOBS AND DUTIES: HOW TO GET READY FOR ASSESSMENT TIME

Planning for charges begins a long time before charge time, particularly in the event that you have a side hustle. Side hustles dislike 9-5 positions. Nobody is taking out charges every check. Hell, with many side hustles, customary checks basically are not piece of the arrangement.

Regardless of whether your second job is working a seasonal work it's basically an assurance your manager isn't taking sufficiently out charges. According to a finance point of view, they view the cash they pay you as the main cash you make, it are probably going to mean they taking out practically zero cash for your charges. It depends on you to intentionally have your 9-5 boss take out extra cash from your duties or to save cash in a bank account in case you get hit with a major duty bill.

In the event that you have second job pay from provisional labor or a business and hope to make more than $1,000 in pay in guaranteed fiscal year, you are expected to cover quarterly assessed charges. Quarterly assessed charges require some mystery, as side hustle pay can vacillate and your different funds moreover influence the amount you owe (for example allowances, pay from your 9-5, and so forth.).

To get the full expense esteem out of your side hustle, it's significant to keep brilliant records of your pay and costs. Whether you keep duplicates of checks and receipts in an envelope or keep everything in a Succeed Bookkeeping sheet, you want to see as a framework that works for you.

One thing I would strongly suggest is opening a different financial record for your part time job. This helps keep your individual and business funds independent and will make following only a tad bit simpler.

For my part time job, I utilize both Google Docs and Succeed to follow what's more, accommodate my funds. I likewise use PayPal and a little business financial records, and try not to have any of my deals hit my own financial records. On the off chance that I need to take a "profit" from my side hustle, I shift cash from my business checking to my own. It makes it much more straightforward to return and accommodate my funds come charge time.

CHAPTER 11

ARRANGING EVERYTHING

Up to this point we've gone over what to do prior to beginning a side hustle, how to track down the right side hustle for you, thoughts for beginning part time jobs, and second job "hacks" that allow your side hustle a superior opportunity of succeeding.

In this part, I need to zero in on two significant themes: staying with a second job and choosing when to momentarily stop.

While beginning a side hustle is an extraordinary initial step, actually over the long run the engaging quality of a side hustle could wear off. You could get worn out from your part time job, lose interest, or begin addressing whether you ought to proceed with your second job. Another quandary that happens to many individuals who part time job is choosing when to leave their ongoing second job for another open door.

STAYING WITH A SIDE HUSTLE

In the writing for a blog world, there is an overall agreement that a greater part of bloggers quit inside the initial a half year. I don't know anybody has at any point really demonstrated this, however it is by all accounts genuinely precise.

There are a couple of reasons this occurs. At first, writing for a blog is a tomfoolery and glitzy thing to seek after. It's possible whenever the individual first has at any point begun a blog. There are fun new highlights and, unimaginably, there are a modest bunch of individuals really visiting the blog!

Over the long run, however, it turns into a toil. Continually concocting new points, organizing with different bloggers, overseeing online entertainment, managing specialized issues, and other work that accompanies possessing a blog becomes baffling and dreadful like it was at the outset. Furthermore, blog traffic is reasonable going up leisurely and there is a virtual assurance that the blog is making pennies daily, if that.

So bloggers quit. What might bloggers at any point do any other way to allow themselves a superior opportunity of moving beyond the half year point? Everything revolves around readiness.

HAVING A STRATEGY PRIOR TO BEGINNING

This might sound dull, yet it can't be put into words: have an arrangement prior to beginning a part time job. In the event that you don't have an arrangement, your possibilities staying with a part time job long haul are low.

A things to ponder while making your arrangement are:

How long do I anticipate doing this side hustle?

- Half year? Endlessly?
- Will I drop this side hustle on the off chance that a more appealing open door goes along?

What is my definitive objective with this part time job?

- Make another revenue stream to balance obligation installments?
- Save x dollars for a particular objective (for example trip abroad)?
- Possibly start another profession?
- Bring in sufficient cash to leave my place of employment?

How long each week will this part time

job take?

- Do I have limit with respect to this second job?
- How might I respond on the off chance that this second job requires surprisingly hours out of each week?

How might I save time for this side hustle? How might I set up my timetable to oblige this side hustle?

How long am I focusing on this side hustle before I will permit myself to consider stopping?
- On the off chance that I don't bring in cash by _____ I will consider stopping
- I will stay with this part time job for _____ months prior to considering stopping.

For what reason would you say you are truly searching for a second job?

How might this part time job help me in different aspects of my life?

Is this second job taking advantage of my natural abilities?

Will I partake in this second job? Is there a

second job I could appreciate more?

Does this second job struggle with my 9-5?

- Will it at any point struggle according to a timing viewpoint?
- Is there any possible irreconcilable situation with this side hustle?

What potential open doors do I trust will emerge from this side hustle?
How might I create those open doors almost certain?

Thoroughly considering the reason why you are beginning a side hustle, how you will make it work, and what your definitive objective is, are extremely significant things to perceive and ponder prior to beginning a second job. Keep in mind, the objective here is to allow your part time job the best opportunity of succeeding. On the off chance that you don't have any idea what your objectives are for your second job, it will be hard to perceive regardless of whether you are fruitful, and particularly troublesome perceiving justifications for why you were or alternately were not successful.

I used to peruse a blog summoned Convey Obligation where the blogger's objective with his side hustle was to convey pizzas on top of his regular occupation to settle obligation forcefully. From what I read, it appeared to be a troublesome undertaking, as he was removing time from his family and forfeiting rest to make his side hustle a triumph. He at last was effective in taking care of his obligation through the expanded pay and I can't resist the urge to think he had the option to continue on the grounds that he knew precisely exact thing he was attempting to achieve with his part time job.

KNOW WHEN TO STOP

You can go through years making arrangements for something yet have it not sort out the manner in which you imagined it. The issue with arranging is that it depends on suspicions, and a portion of those suppositions will undoubtedly change.

Maybe you expected that you would be at similar work the following three years, yet you wind up finding another line of work that requires 10-20 additional hours of your time each week...and those were the 10-20 hours per week you had moved toward adding to your second job.

Presently what do you do? Do you stop? Do you change your part time job?

Some of the time the response is self-evident. In the event that you recently worked 7-4 and, worked a temporary work 6-9, however are presently trapped in the workplace as late as 6pm on occasion, your seasonal work part time job probably will not be reasonable.

Different times, the response is more subtle. At the point when I moved from corporate bookkeeping to corporate money, I needed to offer additional significant investment towards my regular work. Rather than leaving my blog (which I believe is a horrendous thought for a laid out blog, particularly a productive one) I reevaluated a greater amount of the composition. I actually handled all the promoting bargains, altered the posts, and oversaw online entertainment, yet removing composing from the situation saved a significant investment to put towards different pursuits.

Two things I think you really want to consider prior to stopping a side hustle are: what is being offered up as a trade off for stopping? what's more, are there choices for changing your side hustle in a manner that permits you to proceed?

WHAT IS BEING SACRIFICED WHEN YOU QUIT A SIDE HUSTLE?

There was a moment where I thought about selling my blog. At the time I wasn't having a great time running it as I used to, and was a piece worn out from contributing to a blog. I likewise needed to seek after a few different open doors in my extra time.

Selling my blog would have required a ton of work in itself. I would have needed to make definite documentation of all client accounts, financials, publicist connections, from there, the sky is the limit. Having been in the blogosphere for a long while, I realize that there were various upgrades that I could execute that would have very quickly made the webpage more significant.

So I didn't sell and kept on working it as I had been for the past three years.

I'm happy I did. Since postponing selling my blog, I've landed two huge promoting manages significant brands. I likewise was offered the chance to compose this book which could never have been conceivable assuming I had sold my site. By not selling, I kept on presenting myself to the potential gain of significant publicizing bargains, a book arrangement, and that's just the beginning.

The guide I'm attempting toward outline is that you need to truly take some real time to consider what you are surrendering when you quit a second job. The pay you get from your part time job is ordinarily not all you are surrendering. You are additionally surrendering the potential gain that accompanies your side hustle. Obviously, that additionally implies you are not acquiring valuable "available energy" that is probable spurring you to consider stopping in any case.

HOW MIGHT YOU CHANGE/ADJUST YOUR SIDE HUSTLES?

Assuming that you're thinking about stopping your side hustle, it's essential to initially assess how you can change your part time job to be more obliging to your timetable and way of life.

A few second jobs are more straightforward to stop or put a hold on from than others. On the off chance that you are working a seasonal occupation at a rec center toward the end of the week, it very well may be somewhat simple to require a couple of months off and afterward start once more. With some private venture and online second jobs, force can make it challenging to dial back since, supposing that you stop or quit it might make you pass up a few major open doors that were not far off.

Prior to stopping a second job, I profoundly urge you to not just ponder what you are forfeiting by stopping, yet the way in which you can make your part time job work inside your timetable. Could you at any point rethink any of the work? Might you at any point cut back on the pay you bring back home from your side hustle as a trade-off for having another person take on a portion of the work? Could you at any point scale back your hours and time committed to your second job? Can you get it again in the distance? Do you mind whether you are at absolutely no point ever associated with this second job in the future? All great inquiries to pose to yourself prior stopping.

Stopping a side hustle is certainly not something terrible. Numerous effective side hawkers and business people have stopped their second job or definitely changed their methodology. At times staying with a second job keeps you from making the most of more worthwhile or satisfying open doors. Gauge the upsides and downsides and pay attention to your gut feelings.

CONCLUSIVE NOTE

Regardless of whether you are struggling with debt from college, credit cards, or something else, there is a proactive solution you can take to get rid of your debt: side hustles. You can conquer your debt and improve your finances through side hustles.

There are countless people today that are using side hustles to do just that. There's the parents who have started a small business to fund their children's education. There's the new grad who is managing social media accounts of local businesses to offset their student loans. There's the twenty-something that runs a tutoring business on the weekend to pay off their credit card debt.

The options are endless. What will you do?

It's time to hustle away debt.

    "Please Rate And Drop a Review"
    Thanks

OTHER BOOKS BY LILLIAN J. JOHNSON

- 1000 you need to tell your kids before it will be too late
- Secrets to Success
- Why Abortion? 15 ways to protect unwanted Pregnancy
- Cheating Partner; (simple ways to find out if your partner is cheating)
- The 5 exercise to stop Menstrual cramps
- A home not a Prison
- 11 reasons why some people are poor
- Unforgettable Night (A Novel)
- Revenge of the Ghost (A Novel)
- The Last Man on Earth (A Novel)

www.ingramcontent.com/pod-product-compliance
Lightning Source LLC
Chambersburg PA
CBHW052347220526
45465CB00003BA/1000